Neil Dixon

GW00732793

ESSENTIALS

OCR Twenty First Century
GCSE Chemistry A
Revision Guide

Ideas about Science

The OCR Twenty First Century Chemistry specification aims to ensure that you develop an **understanding of science itself** – of how scientific knowledge is obtained, the kinds of evidence and reasoning behind it, its strengths and limitations, and how far we can rely on it.

These issues are explored through Ideas about Science, which are built into the specification content and summarised over the following pages.

The tables below give an overview of the Ideas about Science that can be assessed in each unit and provide examples of content which support them in this guide.

Unit A171 (Modules C1, C2 and C3)

Ideas about Science	Example of Supporting Content
Data: their importance and limitations	Measuring Pollutants (page 5)
Cause–effect explanations	Effects of Pollutants (page 8)
Developing scientific explanations	Geological Processes (page 20)
The scientific community	Nanotechnology (page 17)
Risk	Assessing the Risk of Chemicals (page 23)
Making decisions about science and technology	Reducing Car Pollution (page 9)

Unit A172 (Modules C4, C5 and C6)

Ideas about Science	Example of Supporting Content
Data: their importance and limitations	Collecting Titration Data (page 57)
Cause–effect explanations	Collision Theory (page 59)
Developing scientific explanations	Properties of Ionic Compounds (page 42)
The scientific community	The Development of the Periodic Table (page 29)
Risk	Hazardous Substances (page 32)
Making decisions about science and technology	Metals and the Environment (page 46)

Unit A173 (Module C7)

Ideas about Science	Example of Supporting Content
Data: their importance and limitations	Evaluating Experimental Results (page 85)
Cause–effect explanations	The Economics of the Haber Process (page 77)
Developing scientific explanations	Making and Breaking Bonds (page 74)
The scientific community	Catalysts (page 66)
Risk	Health and Safety (page 64)
Making decisions about science and technology	Green Chemistry (pages 65–66)

Data: Their Importance and Limitations

Science is built on **data**. Chemists carry out experiments to collect and interpret data, seeing whether the data agree with their explanations. If the data do agree, then it means the current explanation is more likely to be correct. If not, then the explanation has to be changed.

Experiments aim to find out what the '**true**' value of a quantity is. Quantities are affected by **errors** made when carrying out the experiment and **random variation**. This means that the measured value may be different to the true value. Chemists try to **control** all the factors that could cause this uncertainty.

Chemists always take **repeat readings** to try to make sure that they have accurately estimated the true value of a quantity. The **mean** is calculated and is the best estimate of what the true value of a quantity is. The more times an experiment is repeated, the greater the chance that the mean value will be very close to the true value.

The **range**, or spread, of data gives an indication of where the true value must lie. Sometimes a measurement will not be in the zone where the majority of readings fall. It may look like the result (called an '**outlier**') is wrong – however, it doesn't automatically mean that it is. The outlier has to be checked by repeating the measurement of that quantity. If the result can't be checked, then it should still be used.

Here is an example of an outlier in a set of data:

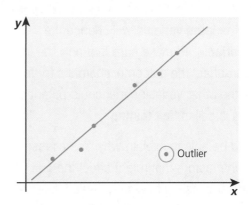

Outlier

(HT) The spread of the data around the mean (the range) gives an idea of whether it really is different to the mean from another measurement. If the ranges for each mean don't overlap, then it's more likely that the two means are different. However, sometimes the ranges do overlap and there may be no significant difference between them.

The ranges also give an indication of reliability – a wide range makes it more difficult to say with certainty that the true value of a quantity has been measured. A small range suggests that the mean is closer to the true value.

If an outlier is discovered, you need to be able to defend your decision as to whether you keep it or discard it.

Ideas about Science

Science is based on the idea that a factor has an effect on an outcome. Chemists make **predictions** as to how the **input variable** will change the **outcome variable**. To make sure that only the input variable can affect the outcome, chemists try to control all the other variables that could potentially alter it. This is called '**fair testing**'.

You need to be able to explain why it's necessary to control all the factors that might affect the outcome. This means suggesting how they could influence the outcome of the experiment.

A **correlation** is where there's an apparent link between a factor and an outcome. It may be that as the factor increases, the outcome increases as well. On the other hand, it may be that when the factor increases, the outcome decreases.

For example, there's a correlation between temperature and the rate of rusting – the higher the temperature, the more rapid the rate of rusting.

Just because there's a correlation doesn't necessarily mean that the factor causes the outcome. Further experiments are needed to establish this. It could be that another factor causes the outcome or that both the original factor and outcome are caused by something else.

The following graph suggests a correlation between going to the opera regularly and living longer. It's far more likely that if you have the money to go to the opera, you can afford a better diet and health care. Going to the opera isn't the true cause of the correlation.

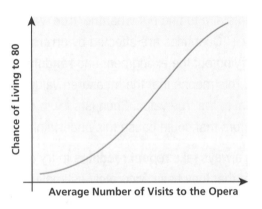

Sometimes the factor may alter the chance of an outcome occurring but doesn't guarantee it will lead to it. The statement 'the more time spent on a sun bed the greater the chance of developing skin cancer' is an example of this type of correlation, as some people will not develop skin cancer even if they do spend a lot of time on a sun bed.

To investigate the link between one **variable** and another variable, chemists have to try to ensure that all other variables are adequately **controlled**. They also have to repeat the experiment and ideally they investigate the link between the variables in other situations and chemical reactions as well. If the link is the same, no matter what reaction is being studied, chemists can be confident about the conclusions they've made about cause and effect.

HT Even so, a correlation and cause will still not be accepted by chemists unless there's a scientific mechanism that can explain them.

Developing Scientific Explanations

Chemists devise **hypotheses** (predictions of what will happen in an experiment), along with an **explanation** (the scientific mechanism behind the hypotheses) and **theories** (that can be tested).

Explanations involve thinking creatively to work out why data have a particular pattern. Good scientific explanations account for most or all of the data already known. Sometimes they may explain a range of phenomena that weren't previously thought to be linked. Explanations should enable predictions to be made about new situations or examples.

When deciding on which is the better of two explanations, you should be able to give reasons why.

Explanations are tested by comparing predictions based on them with data from observations or experiments. If there's an agreement between the experimental findings, then it increases the chance of the explanation being right. However, it doesn't prove it's correct. Likewise, if the prediction and observation indicate that one or the other is wrong, it decreases the confidence in the explanation on which the prediction is based.

The Scientific Community

Once a chemist has carried out enough experiments to back up his/her claims, they have to be reported. This enables the **scientific community** to carefully check the claims, something which is required before they're accepted as scientific knowledge.

Chemists attend **conferences** where they share their findings and sound out new ideas and explanations. This can lead to chemists revisiting their work or developing links with other laboratories to improve it.

The next step is writing a formal **scientific paper** and submitting it to a **journal** in the relevant field. The paper is allocated to **peer reviewers** (experts in their field), who carefully check and evaluate the paper. If the peer reviewers accept the paper, then it's published. Chemists then read the paper and check the work themselves.

New scientific claims that haven't been evaluated by the whole scientific community have less credibility than well-established claims.

It takes time for other chemists to gather enough evidence that a theory is sound. If the results can't be repeated or replicated by themselves or others, then chemists will be sceptical about the new claims.

If the explanations can't be arrived at from the available data, then it's fair and reasonable for different chemists to come up with alternative explanations. These will be based on the background and experience of the chemists. It's through further experimentation that the best explanation will be chosen.

This means that the current explanation has the greatest support. New data aren't enough to topple it. Only when the new data are sufficiently repeated and checked will the original explanation be changed.

(HT) You need to be able to suggest reasons why an accepted explanation will not be given up immediately when new data, which appear to conflict with it, have been published.

Ideas about Science

Risk

Everything we do (or not do) carries **risk**. Nothing is completely risk-free. New technologies and processes based on scientific advances often introduce new risks.

Risk is sometimes calculated by measuring the chance of something occurring in a large sample over a given period of time (**calculated risk**). This enables people to take informed decisions about whether the risk is worth taking. In order to decide, you have to balance the **benefit** (to individuals or groups) with the **consequences** of what could happen.

For example, deciding whether or not to add chlorine to drinking water involves weighing up the benefit (of reducing the spread of cholera) against the risk (of a toxic chlorine leak at the purification plant).

Risk which is associated with something that someone has chosen to do is easier to accept than risk which has been imposed on them.

HT Perception of risk changes depending on our personal experience (**perceived risk**). Familiar risks (e.g. using bleach without wearing gloves) tend to be under-estimated, whilst unfamiliar risks (e.g. making chlorine in the laboratory) and invisible or long-term risks (e.g. cleaning up mercury from a broken thermometer) tend to be over-estimated.

For example, many people under-estimate the risk that adding limescale remover and bleach to a toilet at the same time might produce toxic chlorine gas.

Governments and public bodies try to assess risk and create **policy** on what is and what isn't acceptable. This can be controversial, especially when the people who benefit most aren't the ones at risk.

Making Decisions about Science and Technology

Science has helped to create new technologies that have improved the world, benefiting millions of people. However, there can be unintended **consequences** of new technologies, even many decades after they were first introduced. These could be related to the impact on the environment or to the quality of life.

When introducing new technologies, the potential benefits must be weighed up against the risks. Sometimes unintended consequences affecting the environment can be identified. By applying the scientific method (making hypotheses, explanations and carrying out experiments), chemists can devise new ways of putting right the impact. Devising **life cycle assessments** helps chemists to try to minimise unintended consequences and ensure sustainability.

Some areas of chemistry could have a high potential risk to individuals or groups if they go wrong or if they're abused. In these areas the Government ensures that regulations are in place.

The scientific approach covers anything where data can be collected and used to test a hypothesis. It can't be used when evidence can't be collected (e.g. it can't test beliefs or values).

Just because something can be done doesn't mean that it should be done. Some areas of scientific research or the technologies resulting from them have **ethical issues** associated with them. This means that not all people will necessarily agree with it.

Ethical decisions have to be made, taking into account the views of everyone involved, whilst balancing the benefits and risks. It's impossible to please everybody, so decisions are often made on the basis of which outcome will benefit most people. Within a culture there will also be some actions that are always right or wrong, no matter what the circumstances are.

Ideas about Science

Sample Questions

These sample questions and model answers will help you to prepare for aspects of Ideas about Science in your exam. Some of the exam practice questions in this guide (e.g. questions 2 and 3 on pages 26–27) will also help you to prepare for these types of question.

1. Many people are worried about global warming but there are still some politicians who deny that carbon dioxide produced by human activity is causing global warming. The graph shows how the amount of carbon dioxide in the atmosphere on a remote island in the Pacific Ocean has changed. It also shows how mean air temperature has changed.

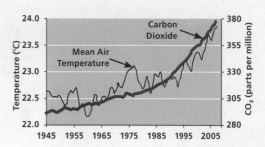

   (a) Describe the correlation between the amount of carbon dioxide in the atmosphere and the mean air temperature. [1]

   As the amount of carbon dioxide increased, so did the mean air temperature.

   (b) The politicians who do not believe in global warming say that this correlation does not prove a cause-and-effect link between carbon dioxide and global warming. Explain the difference between correlation and cause-and-effect. Use the graph to illustrate your answer. [6]

   🖊 *The quality of written communication will be assessed in your answer to this question.*

   A correlation is when a change in the measured factor (outcome variable) occurs at the same time as a change in another factor (input variable). The graph shows that the rise in air temperature happened at the same time and at a similar rate to the increase in carbon dioxide. However, correlation doesn't necessarily indicate a causal link. A cause-and-effect relationship needs a plausible mechanism that explains how the input factor causes the outcome. Scientists would try to perform controlled experiments to show that other factors were not causing the carbon dioxide and air temperature to rise at the same time.

   (c) A group of scientists perform an experiment which suggests that the rise in carbon dioxide levels does cause the increase in air temperature. Why is it important that their ideas are shared with other scientists? [1]

   So that they can be peer reviewed.

   (d) Many scientists say that governments should make new laws to reduce the carbon dioxide released from power stations and that money should be invested in renewable sources of energy. Suggest why governments might be reluctant to do this. [2]

   It could increase the cost of electricity and reduce employment in power stations. The renewable energy sources might not be able to meet the energy demands of the population and there may be risks with the new technologies.

2. Iodine is an important chemical in our diets because it is an essential element in some hormones. In some countries, iodine compounds are added to table salt.

   (a) To make iodine supplements to add to salt, Nick thinks he can extract iodine from seawater. He needs to find out how much iodine there is in seawater. Why should Nick test several samples of seawater, collected at different locations on different days? [1]

   To ensure that the value from his experiment is a good measurement of the true value.

   (b) The data that Nick collects are shown below. All measurements are in parts per million (ppm): 0.05; 0.04; 0.05; 0.05; 0.05; 0.06; 0.05; 0.01; 0.06. Which result is an outlier? [1]

   0.01

Contents

Contents

C1 Air Quality

The Atmosphere

The Earth is surrounded by a **thin layer of gases** called the **atmosphere**.

The atmosphere contains…

- about 78% **nitrogen**
- 21% **oxygen**
- 1% **argon** and other **noble gases**
- small amounts of **water vapour**, **carbon dioxide**, and **other gases**.

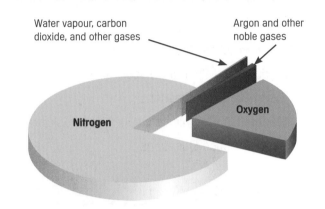

Water vapour, carbon dioxide, and other gases

Argon and other noble gases

Nitrogen

Oxygen

Evolution of the Atmosphere

Scientists believe that the atmosphere probably evolved in the following way:

1 The early atmosphere was created by volcanic activity and consisted mainly of carbon dioxide and water vapour.

2 As the Earth cooled, the water vapour condensed to form the oceans.

3 Simple photosynthetic organisms evolved in the oceans, adding oxygen to the atmosphere and removing carbon dioxide.

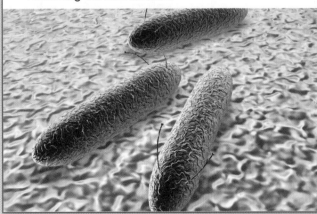

4 Some carbon dioxide was removed due to it dissolving in the oceans and forming **sedimentary rocks** and fossil fuels.

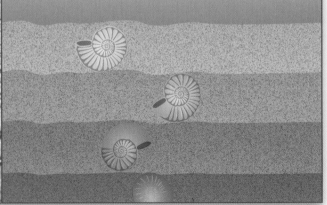

Pollutants in the Air

Pollutants are chemicals. They can harm the **environment** and our **health**.

Human actions, such as burning **fossil fuels**, release pollutants into the **atmosphere**. Power stations and cars release pollutants in this way.

Pollutants can harm us indirectly. For example, **acid rain** makes rivers too acidic for organisms to survive. This affects some **food chains** and **natural resources**, e.g. trees.

Pollutant	Harmful to...	Why?
Carbon dioxide	• Environment	• Traps heat in the Earth's atmosphere (it's a greenhouse gas).
Nitrogen oxides	• Environment • Humans	• Cause acid rain. • Cause breathing problems and can make asthma worse.
Sulfur dioxide	• Environment	• Causes acid rain.
Particulates (small particles of solids, e.g. carbon)	• Environment • Humans	• Make buildings dirty. • Can make asthma and lung infections worse if inhaled.
Carbon monoxide	• Humans	• Prevents the blood from carrying oxygen, which can be fatal.

Measuring Pollutants

It's possible to measure **concentrations** of pollutants in the air in **ppb** (**parts per billion**) or **ppm** (**parts per million**).

For example, a **sulfur dioxide** concentration of 16ppb means that in every one billion (1 000 000 000) molecules of air, 16 molecules will be sulfur dioxide.

When measuring the concentrations of pollutants, it's important to **repeat** the measurements. For example, the concentration of nitrogen oxides from cars (see page 8) may change depending on the

Low Concentration of Pollutants **High Concentration of Pollutants**

The red circles represent pollutant molecules.
Remember that in a gas there are large spaces between molecules.

time of day, the amount of traffic and the weather. Repeat measurements will allow a chemist to calculate a **mean**, which will give a good estimate of the **true value** of the concentration of the pollutant.

Quick Test

1. State the composition of the atmosphere.
2. List the stages involved in the most probable theory of the evolution of the atmosphere.
3. Name two natural processes that remove carbon dioxide from the atmosphere.

Key Words **Pollutant • Acid rain**

C1 Air Quality

Chemicals

Elements are the **'building blocks'** of **all** materials. There are over 100 elements. Each one is made of tiny **particles** called **atoms**.

All atoms of a particular element are the same and **unique** to that element. Atoms can **join together** to form bigger building blocks called **molecules**.

Compounds form when the atoms of two or more different elements **chemically combine**. The properties of compounds are very different from the properties of the elements they're made from.

Chemical symbols and **numbers** are used to write **formulae**. A formula shows the...

- different elements that make up a compound
- number of atoms of each element in one molecule.

Example – A water molecule, H_2O

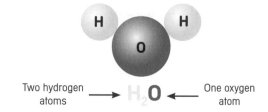

Two hydrogen atoms $\longrightarrow$ H_2O $\longleftarrow$ One oxygen atom

Chemical Change

Chemical reactions form new substances from old ones. Atoms in the **reactants** (starting substances) are rearranged to make **products**:

- Joined atoms may be separated.
- Separate atoms may be joined.
- Joined atoms may be separated and then joined again in different ways.

Usually, these changes **aren't** easily reversible.

Word equations show what happens during a chemical reaction. The **reactants** are on one side and the **products** (newly formed chemicals) on the other:

Reactants $\longrightarrow$ Products

The properties of the products are usually different from the properties of the reactants. No atoms are lost or produced during a chemical reaction, so there will always be the **same number** of atoms on each side.

(HT) Because no atoms are created or destroyed in a chemical reaction, the total mass of the products is the same as the total mass of the reactants. We say that **mass is conserved**.

Combustion

Combustion (burning) is a chemical reaction. Combustion occurs when a fuel reacts with oxygen and energy is released. Because the fuel reacts with oxygen, combustion is a type of **oxidation** reaction. This oxygen usually comes from the air, but fuels burn much faster in pure oxygen.

Coal is mainly made up of **carbon**. The equation opposite shows what happens when coal is burned.

The equation tells us that one atom of carbon (solid) and one molecule of oxygen (gas) produces one molecule of carbon dioxide (gas).

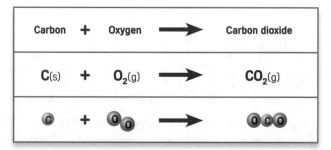

Carbon	+	Oxygen	$\longrightarrow$	Carbon dioxide
$C_{(s)}$	+	$O_2{}_{(g)}$	$\longrightarrow$	$CO_2{}_{(g)}$

Key Words   Element • Atom • Compound • Reactant • Product • Combustion • Oxidation

Complete Combustion

Complete combustion occurs when there's enough oxygen present for a fuel to burn completely. Petrol, diesel and fuel oil consist mainly of compounds called **hydrocarbons** (e.g. methane) which…

- contain only **hydrogen** and **carbon** atoms
- produce carbon dioxide and water (**hydrogen oxide**) when burned in air.

Methane	+	Oxygen	→	Carbon dioxide	+	Water
$CH_4(g)$	+	$2O_2(g)$	→	$CO_2(g)$	+	$2H_2O(l)$

Incomplete Combustion

Incomplete combustion occurs when fuel is burned and there's not enough oxygen. Depending on the amount of oxygen present, **carbon** (C) **particulates** or **carbon monoxide** (CO) may be produced:

Methane	+	Oxygen	→	Carbon	+	Water
$CH_4(g)$	+	$O_2(g)$	→	$C(s)$	+	$2H_2O(l)$

Methane	+	Oxygen	→	Carbon monoxide	+	Water
$2CH_4(g)$	+	$3O_2(g)$	→	$2CO(g)$	+	$4H_2O(l)$

Incomplete combustion occurs in car engines. Exhaust emissions contain carbon particulates and carbon monoxide as well as carbon dioxide.

Coal can contain **sulfur**, so **sulfur dioxide** is released when it's burned:

Sulfur	+	Oxygen	→	Sulfur dioxide
$S(s)$	+	$O_2(g)$	→	$SO_2(g)$

Coal

C1 Air Quality

HT Formation of NO$_x$ Gases

During the combustion of fuels, high temperatures (e.g. in a car engine) can cause **nitrogen** in the atmosphere to **react** with **oxygen**. This produces **nitrogen monoxide (NO)**:

Nitrogen	+	Oxygen	→	Nitrogen monoxide
N_2(g)	+	O_2(g)	→	2NO(g)

Nitrogen monoxide is then **oxidised** to produce **nitrogen dioxide (NO$_2$)**:

Nitrogen monoxide	+	Oxygen	→	Nitrogen dioxide
2NO(g)	+	O_2(g)	→	2NO$_2$(g)

When NO and NO$_2$ occur together they're called **NO$_x$**.

Effects of Pollutants

Once pollutants are released into the **atmosphere** they have to go somewhere because they can't just disappear. This is when they start causing **environmental problems**.

Particulate **carbon** is **deposited** on surfaces such as stone buildings, making them dirty.

Some **carbon dioxide** is removed by **natural processes**:

• It's needed by plants for **photosynthesis**.
• Some **dissolves in rain** and **seawater**, where it **reacts** with other chemicals.

We **produce too much** carbon dioxide, so it's not all used up naturally. It stays in the atmosphere, so carbon dioxide levels **increase** each year.

Experiments show that carbon dioxide is a **greenhouse gas**. It's contributing to global warming, which is leading to **climate change**.

Sulfur dioxide and **nitrogen dioxide** react with water to produce **acid rain**, which damages trees, corrodes metal and upsets the pH balance of rivers, causing plants and animals to die.

It's easy to see this **cause-and-effect relationship** in the laboratory by burning sulfur in oxygen and then dissolving the gas in water. It forms a strongly acidic solution.

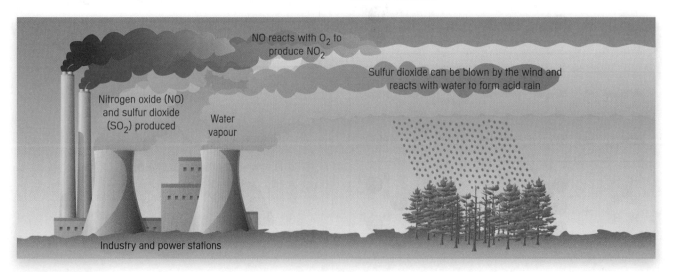

NO reacts with O_2 to produce NO$_2$

Sulfur dioxide can be blown by the wind and reacts with water to form acid rain

Nitrogen oxide (NO) and sulfur dioxide (SO$_2$) produced

Water vapour

Industry and power stations

Atmosphere • Greenhouse gas • Acid rain

Reducing Power Station Pollution

Power station emissions can be reduced by…
- using **less electricity**
- **removing sulfur** and **toxic chemicals** from gas, coal and oil before burning
- using **alternative renewable sources**, e.g. **solar**, **wind** and **hydroelectric** energy

HT • removing sulfur dioxide from flue (chimney) gases by **wet scrubbing** with either a **spray of calcium oxide and water** or using **seawater**.

Reducing Car Pollution

About half of the UK's carbon monoxide emissions are produced by road transport.

Car emissions can be reduced by…
- using low-sulfur fuel in a car with a modern fuel-efficient engine
- **legal limits** for **exhaust emissions**, enforced by MOT (Ministry of Transport) tests
- using public transport
- making sure cars have **catalytic converters**, which reduce carbon monoxide and nitrogen monoxide in the engine exhaust gases.

The equations opposite show the reactions that occur in a catalytic converter.

The only way to reduce emissions is to **burn fewer** fossil fuels. This is very hard because the population of the world is increasing every year and the demand for energy increases all the time.

HT Electricity can be an alternative energy source for cars, but it must be produced renewably. **Biofuels** can be used instead of fossil fuels, but they use up valuable farmland.

Carbon monoxide	+	Oxygen	→	Carbon dioxide
$2CO_{(g)}$	+	$O_{2(g)}$	→	$2CO_{2(g)}$

Nitrogen monoxide	+	Carbon monoxide	→	Nitrogen	+	Carbon dioxide
$2NO_{(g)}$	+	$2CO_{(g)}$	→	$N_{2(g)}$	+	$2CO_{2(g)}$

Quick Test

1. Explain why combustion is a type of oxidation reaction.
2. What does the term 'hydrocarbon' mean?
3. Give three ways to reduce pollution from power stations.
4. Give four ways to reduce pollution from cars.
5. HT Explain how NO_x gases are formed.

1 The graph shows how the concentration of sulfur dioxide in a city centre changed from 1990 to 2010.

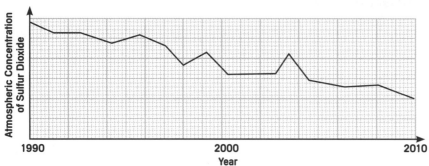

(a) Describe the trend shown by the graph. **[2]**

....

....

....

....

(b) Which of the following factors might be causes of the change in sulfur dioxide shown by the graph? Put ticks (✓) in the boxes next to the **three** correct answers. **[3]**

An increase in the number of cars bought ☐

The introduction of congestion charging in the city centre ☐

A rise in the number of people living in the city ☐

More cars were fitted with catalytic converters ☐

Public transport ticket prices increased ☐

Laws were passed to reduce the amount of sulfur in petrol and diesel ☐

(c) Describe how the burning of a fuel in a power station leads to acid rain. **[3]**

....

....

(d) Nitrogen oxides also contribute to acid rain. Describe how a car engine produces nitrogen oxides. **[2]**

....

....

2 The majority of atmospheric scientists agree on how the Earth's atmosphere is likely to have evolved. Much of their evidence comes from the composition of rocks that were formed millions of years ago.

(a) Explain why scientists can't be totally sure about what the composition of the Earth's early atmosphere was like. **[1]**

....

(b) Which of the following are **two** gases that scientists believe were present in the early atmosphere? Put a (ring) around the correct answers. **[2]**

      oxygen   **nitrogen**   **carbon dioxide**   **water vapour**

(c) Fill in the table below to show the approximate composition of clean, dry air from today's atmosphere. **[3]**

Gas	Percentage
....	78
Oxygen	....
Other gases (mainly argon, with some carbon dioxide)	....

(d) Early organisms on Earth used the Sun's energy to photosynthesise. Describe two changes that the evolution of photosynthetic bacteria and plants had on the Earth's atmosphere. **[2]**

(e) Human activity is affecting the atmosphere more significantly now than at any other time in human history. Name **three** substances that human activity has added to the atmosphere and describe how they're affecting the environment and people's health. **[6]**

    🖉 *The quality of written communication will be assessed in your answer to this question.*

HT 3 A car manufacturer is investing a large amount of money to develop cars that don't rely on fossil fuels. One possibility is to power the car using electricity. Another possibility is to use hydrogen as a fuel.

(a) Describe the most important environmental advantage that hydrogen has over fossil fuels. **[1]**

(b) Describe some of the problems that the manufacturer will need to overcome when developing the hydrogen-fuelled car. **[2]**

C2 Material Choices

Natural and Synthetic Materials

Materials are chemicals, or mixtures of chemicals, e.g. metals, ceramics and polymers. Some materials come from **living things**, e.g. cotton and paper (plants), silk and wool (animals).

Synthetic materials, produced by **chemical synthesis**, can be made as alternatives, starting from materials extracted from the Earth's crust.

For example, the petrochemical industry refines **crude oil** to produce fuels, lubricants and raw materials for chemical synthesis.

Only a small proportion of crude oil is used in chemical synthesis. The majority is used for fuels.

Crude Oil and Fractional Distillation

Crude oil is a raw material found in the Earth's crust. It's a thick black liquid that's made from a mixture of **hydrocarbons**. Hydrocarbons are compounds that are made **only from carbon and hydrogen atoms**. Some hydrocarbons have small molecules but others have much longer chain molecules.

Crude oil is separated by **fractional distillation** into useful **fractions**. The hydrocarbons in a fraction have similar boiling points.

Different fractions have different boiling points, so the fractions in crude oil can be separated by fractional distillation:

1 Crude oil is heated to **evaporate** all of the hydrocarbons.

2 The vapour passes into the fractionating column near the bottom and cools down as it rises.

3 Each fraction **condenses** to a liquid and runs off when it has cooled below its **boiling point**.

4 Any remaining gases leave the tower at the top and are used as gaseous fuels.

Fractional Distillation Tower

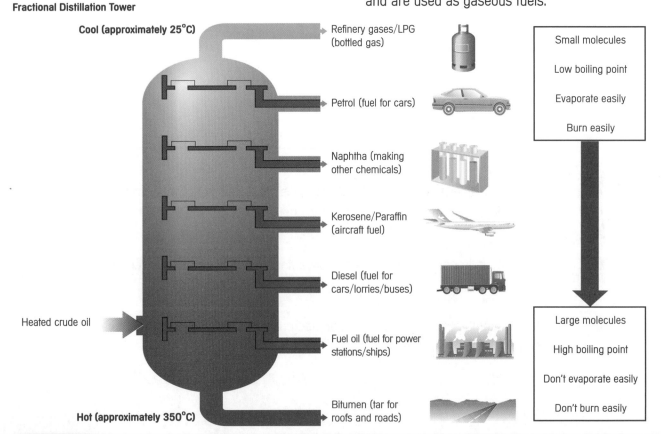

Cool (approximately 25°C)

Refinery gases/LPG (bottled gas)

Petrol (fuel for cars)

Naphtha (making other chemicals)

Kerosene/Paraffin (aircraft fuel)

Diesel (fuel for cars/lorries/buses)

Heated crude oil

Fuel oil (fuel for power stations/ships)

Bitumen (tar for roofs and roads)

Hot (approximately 350°C)

Small molecules
Low boiling point
Evaporate easily
Burn easily

Large molecules
High boiling point
Don't evaporate easily
Don't burn easily

Key Words   Chemical synthesis • Crude oil • Hydrocarbon • Fractional distillation • Fraction

Explaining Boiling Point

All molecules have forces between them that hold the molecules together in a solid or liquid. These forces are called **intermolecular forces**:

1 The longer the hydrocarbon molecules, the stronger these forces are.

2 Stronger intermolecular forces need more energy to overcome them, so a higher temperature is needed to boil the longer hydrocarbon fractions.

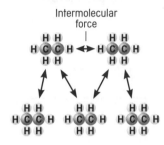

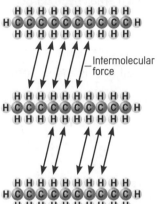

Intermolecular Forces

Small molecules have weak intermolecular forces

Larger molecules have stronger intermolecular forces

Properties of Materials

Different solid materials have different properties. For example, they…

- have different melting points and densities
- can be strong or weak (in tension or compression)
- can be rigid or flexible, hard or soft
- will be better suited to some uses.

The properties of the materials used will affect the durability and effectiveness of a product, so manufacturers test and assess the materials carefully beforehand.

The table below shows the properties and uses of different materials.

Material	Properties	Uses
Unvulcanised rubbers	• Low tensile strength • Soft and flexible / elastic	• Erasers • Rubber bands
Vulcanised rubbers	• High tensile strength • Hard and flexible / elastic	• Car tyres • Conveyor belts • Shock absorbers
Plastic – polythene	• Lightweight (low density) • Flexible and easily moulded	• Plastic bags • Moulded containers
Plastic – polystyrene	• Lightweight (low density) • Stiff • Good thermal insulator as a foam • Water resistant	• Meat trays • Egg cartons • Coffee cups • Protecting appliances and electronics
Synthetic fibres – nylon	• Lightweight (low density) • Tough and waterproof • Blocks ultraviolet light	• Clothing • Climbing ropes
Synthetic fibres – polyester	• Lightweight (low density) • Tough and waterproof	• Clothing • Bottles

C2 Material Choices

Polymerisation

Polymerisation is an important chemical process in which small hydrocarbon molecules (**monomers**) are joined together to make very long molecules (**polymers**).

For example, the polymer poly(ethene), often called polythene, is made from ethene monomers:

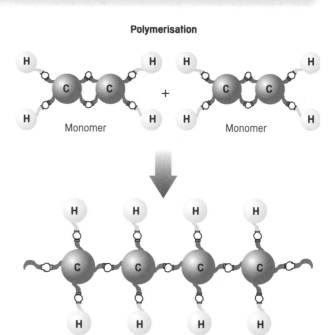

Polymerisation

Monomer + Monomer

Polymer

During a chemical reaction the number of atoms of each element in the products must be the same as in the reactants.

Diagram: Ethene Monomers → Polythene Polymer

Different Monomers Make Different Polymers

By choosing different monomers for the polymerisation process, chemists can produce a range of polymers with different properties. These can then be used for a variety of purposes.

N.B. n is a very large number, indicating that the polymer chain is very long, typically many thousand repeat units long.

Monomer	Polymer	Properties	Uses
Chloroethene (vinyl chloride)	Poly(chloroethene) (Polyvinylchloride or PVC)	Rigid and resistant to ultraviolet light	Window frames
Tetrafluoroethene	Poly(tetrafluoroethene) (PTFE, Teflon)	Very slippery, high melting point and chemically unreactive	Non-stick frying pans

Quick Test

1. Name two natural materials and two synthetic materials.
2. Name the process used to separate crude oil into useful hydrocarbons.
3. Explain the link between molecule size and boiling point.
4. Give a use for kerosene/paraffin.

Polymerisation • Monomer • Polymer

Using Polymerisation

Polymerisation can be used to create a **wide range** of **different materials** which have **different properties**, meaning that they can be used for **different purposes**.

Many traditional (natural) materials have been **replaced** by polymers because of their **superior properties**.

For example, carrier bags used to be made of **paper**. Now they're often made from **polythene** because it's **stronger** and **waterproof**.

Window frames were made of **wood** but are now often made of **polychloroethene** because it's **unreactive** and **doesn't rot**.

Paper Bags

Plastic (Polythene) Bags

Molecular Structure of Materials

Properties of solid materials depend on how their **particles** are arranged and held together.

Natural rubber is a mass of **long-chain molecules**. Atoms within the chains are held together by strong **covalent bonds**, but there are **very weak forces** between the molecules. The long polymer molecules can slide over one another and the material can stretch.

Natural rubber...
- is very **flexible**
- has a **low** melting point because little energy is needed to separate the molecules.

Vulcanised rubber is a mass of tangled molecules where the atoms within the chains are held together by strong covalent bonds. The molecules also have **cross-links**, which are strong covalent bonds between the long-chain molecules.

Vulcanised rubber...
- is quite **rigid** and **hard** to stretch as the molecules won't slide over each other
- needs lots of energy to separate the molecules and has a **high** melting temperature.

Natural Rubber

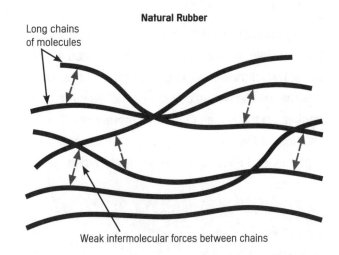

Long chains of molecules

Weak intermolecular forces between chains

Vulcanised Rubber

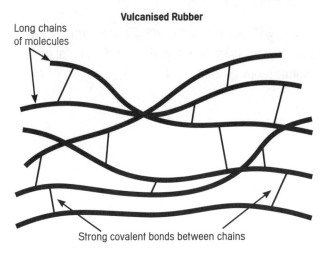

Long chains of molecules

Strong covalent bonds between chains

C2 Material Choices

Modifications in Polymers

It's possible to produce a wide range of different polymers with properties which make them suited to a particular use.

Modifications can also produce changes to the properties of **polymers**.

Increasing the chain length means that there's more contact and therefore stronger forces between the molecules, which makes the plastic stronger.

Cross-links are formed by atoms **bonding** between polymer molecules, so they can no longer move. This makes a **harder**, stronger and stiffer material.

An example of cross-linking is **vulcanisation**, when sulfur atoms form cross-links between rubber molecules. Vulcanised rubber is used to make car tyres and conveyor belts.

Adding **plasticizers** makes a polymer **softer** and **more flexible**. A plasticizer is a small molecule that sits between molecules and forces the chains apart. This means the forces between the chains are **weaker**, so molecules can move more **easily**. **Plasticized PVC** is used in children's toys, and **unplasticized PVC** (uPVC) in window frames.

(HT) A polymer can also be modified by packing molecules more **closely** together to form a **crystalline** polymer.

The intermolecular forces are slightly stronger so the polymer is **stronger**, **denser** and has a slightly **higher** melting point.

uPVC is Used in Window Frames

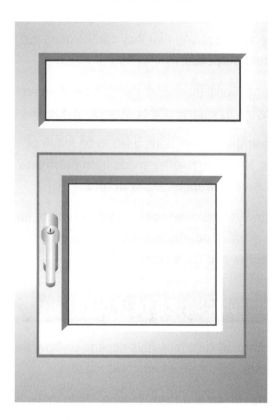

Plasticizers

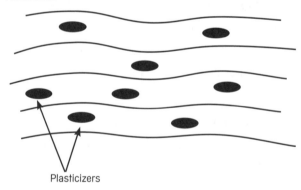

Plasticizers

A Crystalline Polymer

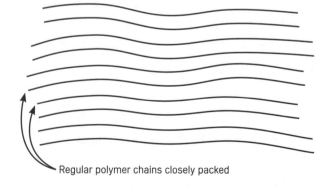

Regular polymer chains closely packed

Key Words Plasticizer • Crystalline

Nanoscale Materials

A **nanometre** is one millionth of a millimetre. This is the width of a few atoms.

Nanoscale particles can...
- occur naturally, e.g. in sea spray
- occur as an accidental result of human activity, e.g. particulate carbon released when fuels burn
- be made deliberately by scientists – this is called **nanotechnology**.

Nanoscale particles have different **properties** to larger particles. This is often because the smaller particles have a much larger **surface area**.

Nanotechnology

Nanotechnology is the production, study and control of tiny particles on a **nanoscale** (1 to 100 nanometres).

Nanoparticles can be used to modify the properties of other materials, especially polymers. Here are two examples:
- Silver nanoparticles can be used to give fibres in clothes **antibacterial** properties. This can help to stop your socks from smelling!
- Adding carbon nanotubes to sports equipment like tennis rackets and golf clubs can make them lighter, stiffer and stronger.

Nanotechnology is a very new science. Some people are worried that these new materials haven't been thoroughly tested and could lead to health problems in the future.

It would be easy for a scientist who has developed a new material made from nanoparticles to say that it's completely safe for the public to use. However, claims made by any one scientist are **critically evaluated** by other scientists before they are accepted by the scientific community.

Quick Test

1. What is the effect on the properties of a plastic of cross-linking the polymer molecules?
2. What is a plasticizer and what does it do to the properties of a polymer?
3. What is nanotechnology?
4. Give an example of how nanoparticles can occur naturally.

C2 Exam Practice Questions

1. Clothing can be made from natural and synthetic materials.

   (a) Name two natural materials that can be used to make clothing. **[2]**

   ....

   ....

   The table below contains information on three different polymers. Use the information to answer the questions that follow.

Polymer	Properties
PTFE	Can be made into flexible sheets that allow water vapour through but not liquid water.
PCBD	Can be made into thick but flexible sheets of rubbery foam.
PAF	Can be made into rigid sheets that are extremely resistant to abrasion.
HDPE	Can be made into flexible waterproof sheets.

   (b) Which polymer should be used to make a wetsuit for winter surfing?
   Put a ring around the correct answer. **[1]**

   PTFE   **PCBD**   **PAF**   **HDPE**

   (c) A police officer needs different clothing depending on the duties that he or she is doing. Sometimes police officers need to work outside in the rain in 'safe' situations for long periods of time. Sometimes they need to be protected from stab injuries.

   Which polymers from the table above would be most appropriate for their clothing in these two different situations? You should justify your choices. **[6]**
   🖉 *The quality of written communication will be assessed in your answer to this question.*

   ....

   ....

   ....

   ....

   ....

   ....

   ....

   (d) In recent years, scientists have researched the effects of adding nanoparticles to materials. Give an example of how nanoparticles have improved the properties of an everyday product. **[2]**

   ....

   ....

2 James has been studying how crude oil is processed to make it more useful. He knows that the first process is called fractional distillation, but he's not sure how it works. Three friends have offered him the following help:

Megan
The longer hydrocarbons condense lower down the tower where it's coldest.

Hannah
The longer molecules have higher boiling points because the forces between the molecules are stronger.

Rob
Smaller molecules need more energy to boil them, so they come off at the top of the tower.

(a) Which of the students has given James correct advice? **[1]**

(b) Name a fraction from crude oil that's not used as a fuel and state what it's used for. **[2]**

HT **3** This question is about polymerisation.

(a) Explain what's meant by the term **polymerisation**. **[2]**

(b) The property of a polymer can be modified in several ways. Describe **two** ways in which this can be achieved and suggest the effect of each modification on the properties of the polymer. **[4]**

C3 Chemicals in Our Lives: Risks and Benefits

Britain's Minerals

Like many countries around the world, Britain has a number of valuable **mineral** deposits in the ground. These include coal, limestone and salt.

Deposits of these minerals were discovered in the north west of England. This led to the development of a successful chemical industry there.

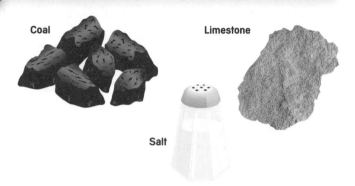

Coal

Limestone

Salt

Geological Processes

Geologists can't know for sure how the surface of the Earth has changed. But they can make suggestions which are supported by evidence from processes that can be seen today. Examples of these processes include…

- mountain building
- **erosion**
- **sedimentation**
- dissolving
- **evaporation**.

Geologists also use **magnetic clues** in rocks to track the very slow movement of the continents over the surface of the Earth. Rocks that now make up parts of Britain were formed in different climates.

Sedimentary rocks often contain clues that suggest how they were formed. These clues include…

- fossils and the presence of shell fragments
- ripple patterns on sediments that settled on the bottom of the sea or a river
- the shape of water-borne grains compared with air-blown grains.

The tectonic plates that make up the Earth's surface are moving, but very slowly. They are dragged by convection currents in the mantle beneath them. This theory is supported by the fact that…

- the continents that we see today seem as though they might have once fitted together
- similar rocks have been found on opposite sides of the Atlantic Ocean.

A Fossil of a Dinosaur

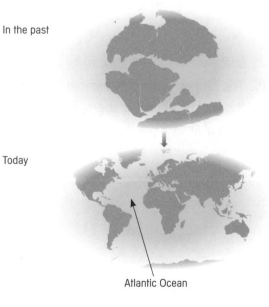

How the Continents Have Moved

In the past

Today

Atlantic Ocean

Key Words   **Mineral • Erosion • Sedimentation • Evaporation**

The Importance of Salt

Salt (**sodium chloride**) is used…

- in the food industry
- as a source of chemicals
- to treat icy roads in winter.

Salt is added to food as a flavouring and a preservative. Too much salt in your diet can lead to high blood pressure and other circulatory conditions.

You need to be able to interpret data about health and salt in food. Look at the data in the table. Which crisps would you recommend to someone with high blood pressure?

Nutritional Information (g per 100g of crisps)	PKT-1 (Ready Salted)	Organic Choice (Plain)	Seaside Choice (Salt and Vinegar)
Protein	7.0	6.0	6.5
Carbohydrate	54.0	61.8	58.6
Fat	30.0	24.0	27.0
Fibre	6.9	8.0	6.1
Salt	2.1	0.2	1.8

Organic Choice would be the most suitable crisps for someone with high blood pressure because they have the lowest salt content.

The **Foods Standards Agency** (FSA) is an independent food safety watchdog that has a role in…

- carrying out risk assessments on chemicals in food
- advising the public about the effect of food on health.

Extracting Salt

Salt can be obtained by evaporating seawater or from solid deposits in the ground. Underground salt deposits can be extracted by…

- mining the solid (often called **rock salt**)
- pumping water into the salt deposit and extracting the solution of salt (called **brine**).

Salt used for roads is more useful if it's extracted as a solid mixed in with grit and sand.

If the salt is to be purified for the chemical or food industry, it might be more efficient to extract it as a solution because this will leave insoluble minerals behind.

Extracting salt can affect the environment.

For example…

- dissolving underground salt deposits using water can lead to the ground above subsiding and buildings possibly collapsing
- salt waste can affect plants and animals by drying them up, through the process of **osmosis**.

Quick Test

1. Name three mineral resources found in Britain.
2. Name three processes that have been involved in creating Britain's mineral resources.
3. State two things that salt is used for.
4. Why is excessive salt in the diet bad for you?

Key Words   Sodium chloride • Brine • Osmosis

C3 Chemicals in Our Lives: Risks and Benefits

Uses of Alkalis

For many years, alkalis have been used for...
- neutralising acidic soils
- making chemicals that bind dyes to cloth
- making soaps from fats and oils
- making glass.

In the past, alkalis were extracted from burnt wood or stale urine. During the Industrial Revolution in the 19th century, more alkali was needed.

HT Remember that soluble hydroxides and carbonates are alkalis and will therefore **neutralise** acids. You also need to know the patterns in the reactions of these alkalis with acids – see Module C6, page 52.

Early Attempts at Making Alkalis

The first process for making alkali from salt and limestone, using coal as a fuel, had a big effect on the environment:
- Lots of acidic hydrogen chloride gas was released.
- Large waste heaps were made.
- The waste heaps decomposed to release toxic and foul-smelling hydrogen sulfide gas.

Some of these waste products can be turned into useful materials. For example, hydrogen chloride can be **oxidised** to make chlorine.

The Modern Chlor-alkali Industry

Chlorine, **hydrogen** and the very important alkali **sodium hydroxide** are now extracted from **brine** (salt water) using **electrolysis**. Electrolysis occurs when an electric current is used to split up a liquid or dissolved compound (called the **electrolyte**).

The environmental impact of the industrial electrolysis of brine is carefully monitored because chlorine is toxic, sodium hydroxide is corrosive and hydrogen is flammable.

Electrolysis of Sodium Chloride Solution (Brine)

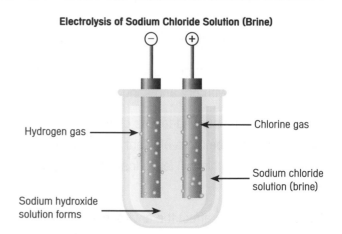

Hydrogen gas

Chlorine gas

Sodium chloride solution (brine)

Sodium hydroxide solution forms

Uses of the Products from Brine

Sodium hydroxide...

- is an important alkali
- is used to make soaps, detergents, paper and textiles
- is used as a domestic drain cleaner
- is a corrosive substance.

Hydrogen...

- is a flammable gas
- is used in processing hydrocarbon fuels, making margarine and making ammonia in the Haber process
- will be used as a clean fuel in the future.

Chlorine...

- can be used as a bleach
- can be used to kill bacteria in drinking water – this has controlled many diseases in humans around the world
- is a toxic gas.

You may be asked to interpret data on the use of chlorine.

Some people are concerned about the possible disadvantages of adding chlorine to drinking water. Chlorine might react with organic (carbon-based) chemicals in the water to produce small amounts of harmful chemicals.

Chlorine can also be used to make the polymer PVC, which is often plasticized. Over time, the plasticizer molecules can leach out and harm the environment.

Assessing the Risk of Chemicals

Many chemical industries are well regulated. However, there are a large number of industrial chemicals with a variety of uses that haven't been risk assessed thoroughly. Some of these chemicals may be dangerous for humans or for the environment.

Chemicals can be very dangerous for a variety of reasons:

- They last in the environment for a very long time.
- They can be carried long distances in the atmosphere, rivers and oceans.
- They can accumulate in food chains and animal tissues.

When assessing the risk of using a chemical, we often estimate the **chance of being hurt** and the **severity of the consequences** if we do get hurt.

People are often more likely to take risks when the effects are short lived rather than long term, and when they have a choice about using a chemical, rather than being forced to use it.

Life Cycle of a Product

New products must undergo a **life cycle assessment** (LCA), which has four phases:

- Making the material from natural raw materials
- Manufacture
- Use
- Disposal.

Each part of the life cycle is assessed for its **environmental impact** by the amount of **energy** and **resources** that will be used, and how materials will be **obtained** and **disposed** of.

The purpose of an LCA is to help find the most **sustainable** method so that current needs are met without damaging resources for the future.

Factors to be Assessed in an LCA

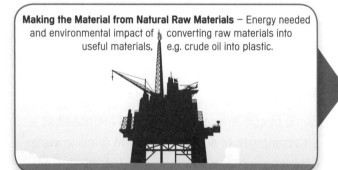

Making the Material from Natural Raw Materials – Energy needed and environmental impact of converting raw materials into useful materials, e.g. crude oil into plastic.

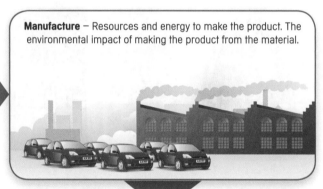

Manufacture – Resources and energy to make the product. The environmental impact of making the product from the material.

Disposal – Energy needed to dispose of the product. Environmental impact of landfill, incineration and recycling.

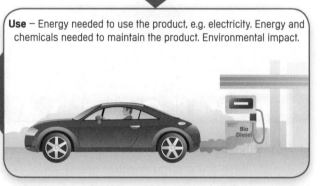

Use – Energy needed to use the product, e.g. electricity. Energy and chemicals needed to maintain the product. Environmental impact.

Materials for a Job

Different materials can perform the **same** job.

For example, disposable nappies are more convenient but an LCA shows that reusable nappies are environmentally better. Evidence in the table shows that reusing nappies uses fewer resources and produces less waste.

Impact per Baby, per Year	Reusable Nappies	Disposable Nappies
Energy needed to produce product	2532MJ	8900MJ
Waste water	12.4m^3	28m^3
Raw materials used	29kg	569kg
Domestic solid waste produced	4kg	361kg

Example – A uPVC Window Frame

Stage of Life Cycle	Energy Requirements Assessment Questions	Environmental Impact Assessment Questions
Making the materials from natural substances	How much energy would be needed... • to drill and distil the oil? • to produce chlorine by electrolysing seawater? • for polymerisation?	• How much oil will be taken from natural reserves? • What is the risk of spillage during transportation? • What is the effect of leaked oil on the atmosphere and ecosystem?
Manufacture	How much energy would be needed... • to mould the window frame? • to transport the materials between stages?	• What pollutants and waste materials are produced during manufacture and transportation?
Use	How much energy would be needed... • to keep the window frames clean?	• How will the product be transported between the factory and home? • What will be the effect of the new window frame on the energy efficiency of the house and the amount of fossil fuel burned to keep the house warm?
Disposal	How much energy would be used or recovered if the window frame was... • recycled? • incinerated? • thrown away?	• Would incineration produce pollutants or toxic gases? • What is the effect of plasticizers leaching out of the PVC and into the environment if thrown away? • What is the energy value of the plastic if incinerated? • How much landfill space will the product take up?

Quick Test

1. Name three products from the electrolysis of brine (salt water).
2. What is meant by the term 'electrolysis'?
3. Give one use of chlorine.
4. Briefly describe what happens in a life cycle assessment.

C3 Exam Practice Questions

1 Sodium chloride is also known as 'common salt'. It has a variety of uses and is also a useful raw material for many chemical processes.

(a) When used as a raw material for the chemical industry, where does sodium chloride come from? **[1]**

_____

(b) Sodium chloride is often added to food. Give one advantage and one disadvantage of adding sodium chloride to food. **[2]**

Advantage:_____

Disadvantage:_____

(c) Sodium chloride solution (brine) can be electrolysed to produce three useful chemicals. Draw straight lines to join the name of the chemical with some of its major uses and one of its hazards. **[4]**

Chemical	Use	Hazard
Hydrogen	Used to make soaps	Flammable
Chlorine	Used in bleaches and plastics	Corrosive
Sodium hydroxide	Used in the production of margarines	Toxic

2 A team of research scientists has developed a new plastic to use for making highly-absorbent nappies. In order to advertise their new substance to companies which manufacture nappies, the scientists need to carry out a life cycle assessment (LCA).

(a) In a life cycle assessment, scientists consider the use of resources, energy input and environmental impact over four stages of a product's life. What are the four stages? **[4]**

_____

_____

_____

_____

(b) Why is it important that the tests completed in an LCA are repeated by another team of scientists? **[1]**

_____

3 Cling film was discovered by accident in 1953 by a scientist who was trying to produce a protective plastic shell for his car. He discovered that he had made a polymer film that stuck to many surfaces but was easy to remove.

(a) Cling film has many properties that make it useful as a covering for food in bowls and on plates. Put ticks (✓) in the boxes next to the **three** properties that make it useful for this purpose. **[3]**

Oxygen can't pass through the film ◻ Water can't pass through the film ◻

Transparent ◻ Doesn't conduct electricity ◻

Low melting point ◻

(b) Cling film was originally made from PVC, which is a polymer that had plasticizers added to it. These are small molecules that increase its flexibility. After a number of years, scientists began to worry that the plasticizers used in cling film might leak out and into foods that were covered in the film. Plasticizers are particularly soluble in fats and oils.

(i) Why might this have been a problem? **[1]**

....

(ii) Suggest what scientists might have advised consumers to do when the concerns over plasticizers were first raised. **[1]**

....

(iii) Suggest how scientists would find out if plasticizers should be banned from use in cling film. **[6]**
✎ *The quality of written communication will be assessed in your answer to this question.*

....

....

....

....

....

....

....

....

HT **4** This question is about two compounds of lithium: lithium hydroxide (LiOH) and lithium carbonate (Li_2CO_3).

(a) What pH would you expect a solution of lithium hydroxide to have? **[1]**

....

(b) Write a word equation showing the reaction between lithium carbonate and hydrochloric acid. **[3]**

....

(c) Write a symbol equation for the reaction between lithium hydroxide and nitric acid (HNO_3). **[2]**

....

C4 Chemical Patterns

The Periodic Table

An **element** is made of only one kind of **atom**. All the atoms of an element have the same number of **protons**.

Different **elements** have different **proton numbers** and they're arranged in order of increasing proton number in the **modern periodic table**. This gives repeating **patterns** in the **properties** of elements.

You can use the periodic table as a reference table to obtain the following information about the elements:

- Relative atomic mass – the total number of protons and **neutrons** in an atom
- Symbol
- Name
- Atomic (proton) number – the number of protons (and also the number of **electrons**) in an atom.

You can also tell if elements are **metals** or **non-metals** by looking at their position in the table.

N.B. You will be given a copy of the periodic table in the exam. You can find one at the back of this book.

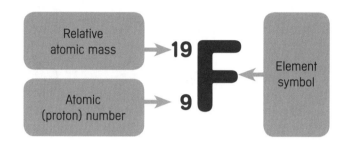

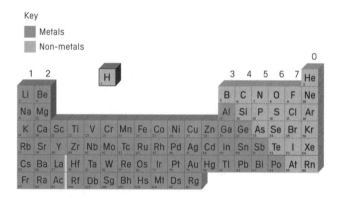

Groups

A **vertical column** of elements is called a **group**. Elements that are in the same group have **similar properties**.

Group 1 elements include…
- lithium (Li)
- sodium (Na)
- potassium (K).

The group number corresponds to the number of electrons in the outer shell of an atom. For example…
- **Group 1** elements have **one electron** in their outer shell
- **Group 7** elements have **seven electrons** in their outer shell.

Periods

A **horizontal row** of elements is called a **period**. Examples of elements in the same period are lithium (Li), carbon (C) and neon (Ne).

The period number corresponds to how many shells there are in an atom of a particular element. For example, elements with three shells are found in the third period.

Key Words   Element • Atom • Proton • Neutron • Electron • Group • Period

The Development of the Periodic Table

Many years ago, scientists identified elements as chemicals that couldn't be broken down. Some scientists tried to find patterns in these elements, but other scientists didn't think that this would be possible.

In 1817, **Döbereiner** realised that some elements with similar properties formed groups of three. He called these **triads**. One example is lithium, sodium and potassium. Another is chlorine, bromine and iodine.

In 1865, **Newlands** suggested that when the elements were arranged in order of increasing atomic weight, some repeating patterns in properties could be seen. He called this the **law of octaves**, after the musical scale. Other scientists thought this was ridiculous.

In 1869, **Mendeleev** presented his periodic table, which is much like the one we use today. His table allowed **similar elements to be grouped together** and also showed the **repeating patterns** that other chemists had noticed.

Mendeleev deliberately left some gaps in his periodic table, which were for elements that he suggested hadn't been discovered yet. He even correctly predicted the properties of these elements.

New technologies have been very important in discovering new elements. For example, **spectroscopy** helped to discover the noble gases, which Mendeleev didn't include in his periodic table because none of them had yet been found.

Atoms

An **atom** has a **small central nucleus**, made up of **protons** and **neutrons**. The nucleus is surrounded by **electrons,** which are arranged in **shells (energy levels)**.

An atom has the same number of protons as electrons, so the atom as a whole is **neutral** (i.e. it has no electrical charge).

A proton has the same **mass** as a neutron. The mass of an electron is **negligible** (nearly zero).

All atoms of the same element have the same number of protons.

HT You can use information from the periodic table to work out the number of protons, electrons and neutrons in any atom. For example, consider $^{19}_{9}F$. The atomic number is the number of protons. In this example, fluorine has nine protons. For the atom to be neutral, it must have the same number of electrons: nine. The mass of the atom is 19, and we know that only protons and neutrons have mass, so the rest of the mass (19 minus 9) must come from neutrons. So fluorine atoms have 10 neutrons.

Atomic Particle	Relative Mass	Relative Charge
Proton	1	+1
Neutron	1	0
Electron	Nearly zero	−1

A Fluorine Atom

Nucleus

Shell

Key: ● Proton ● Neutron ✗ Electron

C4 Chemical Patterns

Spectroscopy

Some elements emit distinctive coloured flames when they're heated:

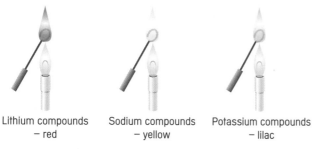

Lithium compounds – red   Sodium compounds – yellow   Potassium compounds – lilac

N.B. You don't need to remember these colours.

The light emitted from the flame of an element produces a characteristic **line spectrum**.

Scientists realised some time ago that each element has its own unique spectrum.

The study of **spectra** has been increasingly used to analyse unknown substances and discover new elements. For example, the line spectrum for helium was first seen in light from the Sun, before it was discovered on Earth.

Electron Configuration

The **electron configuration** of an atom shows how the electrons are arranged in shells around the **nucleus**:

- The electrons in an atom fill up the lowest energy level first. This is the shell closest to the nucleus.
- The first shell can hold up to two electrons.
- The shells after this can hold up to eight electrons.

An electron configuration is written as a series of numbers, e.g. 2.8.1. Going across a **period**, electron configurations increase by one, e.g. sodium 2.8.1, magnesium 2.8.2, aluminium 2.8.3, until the outer shell is full, e.g. argon 2.8.8.

N.B. This is only true for the first 20 elements.

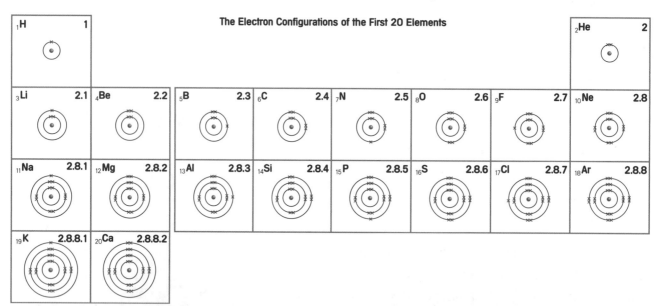

The Electron Configurations of the First 20 Elements

Quick Test

1. Why are lithium, sodium and potassium all found in the same group of the periodic table? Use ideas about their properties and their electron configurations.
2. What is the mass and charge of...
   (a) a proton?   **(b)** an electron?   **(c)** a neutron?

Electron configuration • Nucleus • Period

(HT) Balanced Equations

The total mass of the **products** of a chemical reaction is always equal to the total mass of the **reactants**. This is because **no atoms are lost or made**.

So, chemical symbol equations must always be **balanced**. There must be the same number of atoms of each element on both sides of the equation.

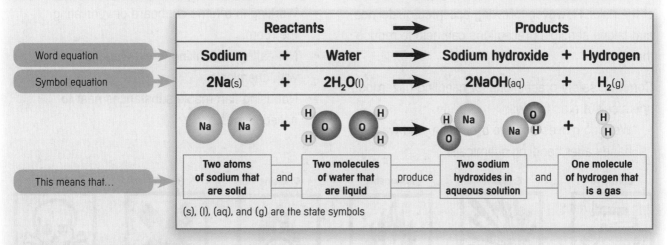

	Reactants				Products		
Word equation	Sodium	+	Water	→	Sodium hydroxide	+	Hydrogen
Symbol equation	$2Na_{(s)}$	+	$2H_2O_{(l)}$	→	$2NaOH_{(aq)}$	+	$H_{2(g)}$

| This means that... | Two atoms of sodium that are solid | and | Two molecules of water that are liquid | produce | Two sodium hydroxides in aqueous solution | and | One molecule of hydrogen that is a gas |

(s), (l), (aq), and (g) are the state symbols

Writing Balanced Equations

Follow these steps to write a balanced equation:
1. Write a word equation for the chemical reaction.
2. Substitute **formulae** for the names of the elements or **compounds** involved.
3. Balance the equation by adding numbers in front of the reactants and/or products.
4. Write a balanced symbol equation.

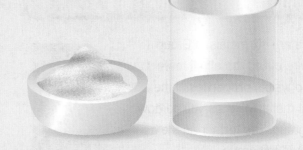

	Reactants			→	Products
1 Write a word equation	Magnesium	+	Oxygen	→	Magnesium oxide
2 Replace with formulae	Mg	+	O_2	→	MgO

3 Balance the equation

- There are two **O**s on the reactant side, but only one **O** on the product side. We need to add another **MgO** to the product side to balance the **O**s.
- We now need to add another **Mg** on the reactant side to balance the **Mg**s.
- There are two magnesium atoms and two oxygen atoms on each side – **it's balanced**.

| 4 Write the balanced symbol equation | $2Mg_{(s)}$ | + | $O_{2(g)}$ | → | $2MgO_{(s)}$ |

C4 Chemical Patterns

Hazardous Substances

Hazards are identified by **symbols** that have specific meanings. When using hazardous chemicals it's impossible to completely remove all of the risks. However, following accepted guidelines and taking sensible precautions can help to reduce the risk.

Common safety precautions for handling hazardous chemicals are as follows:

- Wearing gloves and eye protection, and washing hands after handling chemicals.
- Using safety screens.
- Using small amounts and low concentrations of the chemicals.
- Working in a fume cupboard or ventilating the room.
- Not eating or drinking when working with chemicals.
- Not using flammable substances near to naked flames.

Corrosive	Explosive	Flammable	Oxidising	Harmful	Toxic

Group 1 – The Alkali Metals

There are six metals in Group 1. They're called the **alkali metals**. The physical **properties** of the alkali metals alter as you go down the group. The further an **element** is down the group…

- the **higher** the **reactivity**
- the **lower** the **melting** and **boiling points**
- the higher the density.

Element	Melting Point (°C)	Boiling Point (°C)	Density (g/cm³)
Lithium, Li	180	1340	0.53
Sodium, Na	98	883	0.97
Potassium, K	64	760	0.86
Rubidium, Rb	39	688	1.53
Caesium, Cs	29	671	1.90

(HT) Trends in Group 1

Alkali metals have similar properties because they all have **one electron** in their outer shell.

The alkali metals become **more reactive** as you go down the group because the outer shell gets further away from the influence of the **nucleus** and so the outer electron is **lost more easily**.

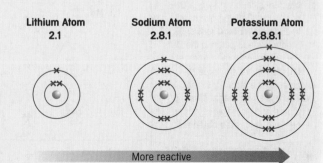

Alkali Metal Compounds

Alkali metals can react to form **compounds**.

Alkali metals are shiny when freshly cut, but they quickly **tarnish in moist air**, go dull and become covered in a layer of metal oxide.

Alkali metals react **vigorously** with **chlorine** to form white crystalline **salts**.

A general equation can be used, where M refers to the alkali metal:

$$2M_{(s)} \ + \ Cl_{2(g)} \ \longrightarrow \ 2MCl_{(s)}$$

For example:

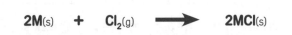

| Lithium | + | Chlorine | | Lithium chloride |

$$2Li_{(s)} \ + \ Cl_{2(g)} \ \longrightarrow \ 2LiCl_{(s)}$$

Alkali metals react with **water** to form a **metal hydroxide** and **hydrogen gas**. The metal hydroxide dissolves in water to form an **alkaline** solution:

$$2M_{(s)} \ + \ 2H_2O_{(l)} \ \longrightarrow \ 2MOH_{(aq)} \ + \ H_{2(g)}$$

N.B. (s) means solid; (l) means liquid; (g) means gas; (aq) means aqueous (dissolved in water)

For example:

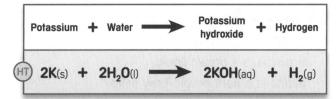

| Potassium | + | Water | | Potassium hydroxide | + | Hydrogen |

(HT) $$2K_{(s)} \ + \ 2H_2O_{(l)} \ \longrightarrow \ 2KOH_{(aq)} \ + \ H_{2(g)}$$

When lithium, sodium and potassium react with cold water they…
- float (due to their low density)
- produce bubbles of hydrogen gas.

The reactivity of alkali metals increases further down the group:
- Lithium reacts quickly with water.
- Sodium reacts more vigorously with water and melts.
- Potassium reacts so vigorously with water that sparks are produced and a purple flame is seen.

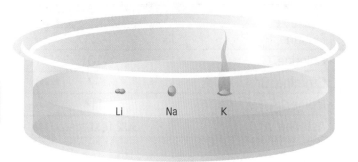

Hazards of Alkali Metals

Alkali metals carry hazard symbols. When working with Group 1 metals, you should…
- use small amounts of the metals
- wear safety glasses and use safety screens
- watch teacher demonstrations carefully
- avoid working near naked flames
- ensure that the metals are stored under oil and that the lids are always tightly secured.

Quick Test

1. Describe the trends in melting point and reactivity as you go down Group 1.
2. Give one reason why the Group 1 elements are called 'alkali metals'.
3. Describe how potassium reacts with cold water.
4. (HT) Why does potassium react faster than sodium?

C4 Chemical Patterns

Group 7 – The Halogens

There are five non-metals in Group 7.

At room temperature and room pressure...
- chlorine is a **green gas**
- bromine is a **brown liquid**
- iodine is a **dark purple/grey solid**.

N.B. Iodine turns into a purple gas when heated.

All **halogens** consist of **diatomic molecules** (they only exist in pairs of **atoms**), e.g. Cl_2, Br_2, I_2.

You can use halogens to **bleach dyes** and **kill bacteria** in water. The physical **properties** of the halogens alter as you go down the group.

The further an element is down the group...
- the **lower** the **reactivity**
- the **higher** the **melting** and **boiling points**
- the **higher** the **density**.

Halogens react with alkali metals to produce **halides**.

Here are some examples:

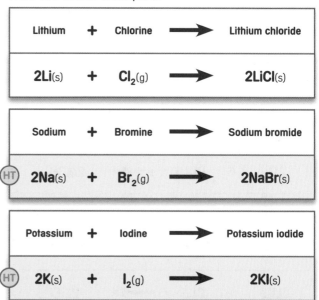

The halogens have similar properties because they all have **seven electrons** in their outer shell.

Halogen	Melting Point (°C)	Boiling Point (°C)	Density (g/cm³)
Fluorine, F_2	-220	-188	0.0016
Chlorine, Cl_2	-101	-34	0.003
Bromine, Br_2	-7	59	3.12
Iodine, I_2	114	184	4.95
Astatine, At_2	302 (estimated)	337 (estimated)	Not known

HT Trends in Group 7

The halogens have similar properties because they all have **seven electrons** in their outer shell.

The halogens become **less reactive** as you go down the group because the outer shell gets further away from the influence of the **nucleus** and so an electron is **less easily gained**.

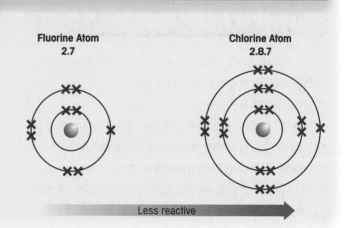

Halogen • Diatomic molecule • Atom

Hazards of Halogens

Halogens carry hazard symbols.

When working with halogens, you should…
- wear safety glasses
- work in a fume cupboard
- make sure the room is well ventilated
- use small amounts of very dilute concentrations
- avoid working near naked flames
- watch teacher demonstrations carefully.

Halogen	Hazard Symbol		
Fluorine, F_2	☠	🔥	⚗
Chlorine, Cl_2	☠	🔥	
Bromine, Br_2	☠	⚗	
Iodine, I_2	✖	🔥	

Displacement Reactions of Halogens

A **more reactive** halogen will **displace** a **less reactive** halogen from an aqueous solution of its salt. This means that chlorine will displace both bromine and iodine, while bromine will displace iodine.

An example is shown opposite.

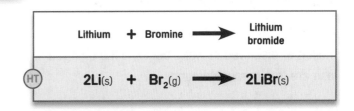

Potassium iodide + Chlorine → Potassium chloride + Iodine

$$2KI_{(aq)} + Cl_{2(aq)} \longrightarrow 2KCl_{(aq)} + I_{2(aq)}$$

Reactions of Halogens with Alkali Metals

Halogens react with other elements to form **compounds**.

Their reactions with alkali metals are highly **exothermic**. They form ionic compounds. An example is shown opposite.

Lithium + Bromine → Lithium bromide

(HT)

$$2Li_{(s)} + Br_{2(g)} \longrightarrow 2LiBr_{(s)}$$

Properties of the Compounds of Halogens with Alkali Metals

Experiments show that **compounds** of alkali metals and halogens **conduct electricity** when they're molten or dissolved in water.

You can conclude from this that they're made up of **charged particles** called **ions**.

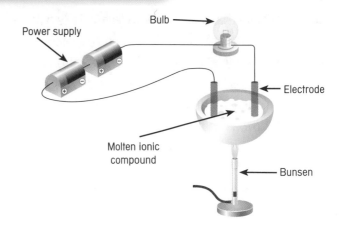

Power supply • Bulb • Electrode • Molten ionic compound • Bunsen

C4 Chemical Patterns

Ions

Ions are **atoms** (or groups of atoms) that have **gained** or **lost electrons**.

As the numbers of **protons** and electrons are no longer equal, ions have an overall charge.

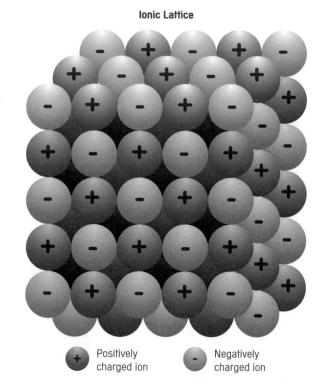

Sodium, Na Atom

Protons = 11
Electrons = 11

Equal number of protons and electrons, so no charge

Sodium, Na⁺ Ion

Protons = 11
Electrons = 10

One more proton, so positive charge

Ionic Bonding

Ionic bonding occurs between a **metal** and a **non-metal**. Electrons transfer from one atom to another to form electrically charged ions:

- Atoms that **lose** electrons become **positively charged ions**.
- Atoms that gain electrons become **negatively charged ions**.

Each ion has a full or empty outer shell of electrons.

Compounds of Group 1 metals and Group 7 **elements** are **ionic compounds** (**salts**). Ionic compounds form **crystals** because the ions are arranged into a **regular lattice**. When ionic crystals melt or dissolve in water, they **conduct electricity**.

Ionic compounds conduct electricity when they're molten or dissolved in water because the charged ions are free to move around.

Ionic Lattice

Positively charged ion

Negatively charged ion

Example 1 – Sodium Chloride

Sodium and chlorine bond ionically to form sodium chloride, NaCl:

1. The sodium (Na) atom has one electron in its outer shell that is transferred to the chlorine (Cl) atom.
2. The sodium (Na) atom has lost one electron and is now a positively charged sodium ion (Na⁺). The chlorine (Cl) atom has gained one electron and is now a negatively charged chloride ion (Cl⁻).
3. Both atoms now have **eight electrons in their outer shell**. The atoms become ions Na⁺ and Cl⁻ and the compound formed is sodium chloride, NaCl.

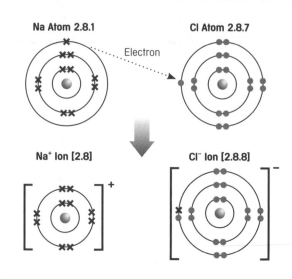

Na Atom 2.8.1

Cl Atom 2.8.7

Electron

Na⁺ Ion [2.8]

Cl⁻ Ion [2.8.8]

Ion • Atom • Electron • Proton • Ionic bond • Compound • Element

Example 2 – Potassium Chloride

Potassium and chlorine bond ionically to form potassium chloride, KCl:

1. The potassium (K) atom has one electron in its outer shell that is transferred to the chlorine (Cl) atom.

2. The potassium (K) atom has lost one electron and is now a positively charged potassium ion (K^+). The chlorine (Cl) atom has gained one electron and is now a negatively charged chloride ion (Cl^-).

3. Both atoms now have **eight electrons in their outer shell**. The compound formed is potassium chloride, KCl.

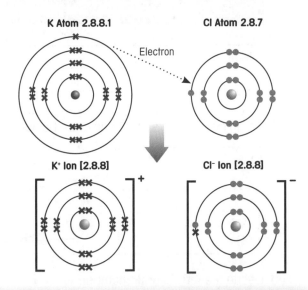

K Atom 2.8.8.1   Cl Atom 2.8.7

Electron

K^+ Ion [2.8.8] Cl^- Ion [2.8.8]

HT Formulae of Ionic Compounds

Ionic compounds are electrically **neutral** substances that have equal amounts of positive and negative charge.

If you know the charge given on both ions you can work out the formula.

For example, Na^+ and Cl^- combine to form NaCl.

If you know the formula and the charge on one of the ions, you can work out the charge on the other ion.

For example, $MgBr_2$ is made up of two Br^- ions that combine with one Mg^{2+} ion.

		Negative Ions	
		1– e.g. Cl^-, OH^-	2– e.g. SO_4^{2-}, O^{2-}
Positive Ions	1+ e.g. K^+, Na^+	KCl 1+ ← → 1– NaOH 1+ ← → 1–	K_2SO_4 2 × 1+ = 2+ → 2– Na_2O 2 × 1+ = 2+ → 2–
	2+ e.g. Mg^{2+}, Cu^{2+}	$MgCl_2$ 2+ → 2 × 1– = 2– $Cu(OH)_2$ 2+ → 2 × 1– = 2–	$MgSO_4$ 2+ → 2– CuO 2+ → 2–
	3+ e.g. Al^{3+}, Fe^{3+}	$AlCl_3$ 3+ → 3 × 1– = 3– $Fe(OH)_3$ 3+ → 3 × 1– = 3–	$Al_2(SO_4)_3$ 2 × 3+ → 3 × 2– = 6+ → = 6– Fe_2O_3 2 × 3+ → 3 × 2– = 6+ → = 6–

Quick Test

1. Which of these is the odd one out and why? Chlorine; lithium; iodine; bromine; fluorine.
2. What happens to the melting point and reactivity of the halogens as you go down the group?
3. What will be the products when bromine is mixed with a solution of potassium iodide?
4. What is the name of the product made when lithium reacts with fluorine?

C4 Exam Practice Questions

1 (a) Complete the table below about sub-atomic particles. **[3]**

Particle	Relative Mass	Relative Charge
....	1	....
Neutron	....	....
....	Negligible	....

(b) Complete the labels on the diagram below. **[2]**

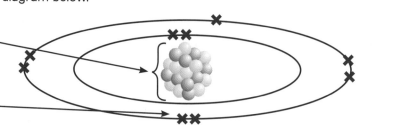

(i) ....

(ii) ....

(c) Define the term **atomic number**. **[1]**

....

(d) Sophie, Catherine and Imran are discussing their understanding of the halogen elements in Group 7 of the periodic table.

Sophie
All of the halogen elements are gases at room temperature.

Catherine
Chlorine reacts with sodium to form a compound called sodium chloride.

Imran
The halogens react in similar ways because they all have seven electrons in their outer shell.

(i) Which of the students is **incorrect**? Put a ring around the appropriate answer. **[1]**

Sophie   **Catherine**   **Imran**

(ii) Write a word equation for the reaction that Catherine is describing. **[2]**

....

2 This question is about the elements in Group 1 of the periodic table.

(a) What name is given to the elements in Group 1? **[1]**

....

(b) Use your knowledge and understanding of the properties of the elements in Group 1 to complete the following table. **[3]**

Element	Melting Point (K)	Boiling Point (K)	Formula of Chloride
Lithium	453	....	LiCl
Sodium	370	1156	....
Potassium	....	1032	KCl

(c) Describe what happens when a piece of sodium is placed in a large bowl of water. Include a word equation for the reaction that occurs and state the pH of the solution that is formed. **[4]**

(d) The following hazard symbol is found on a jar containing sodium. State what it means and describe a safety precaution that you would follow when dealing with any chemical that has this hazard symbol. **[2]**

HT **3** This question is about the element fluorine.

(a) Work out the number of protons, electrons and neutrons in an atom of fluorine. **[3]**

Protons: .... Electrons: .... Neutrons: ....

(b) Fluorine is a diatomic gas and has the formula F_2. Write a balanced symbol equation for the reaction between fluorine and sodium, including state symbols. **[3]**

(c) A student places some solid lead fluoride powder into a beaker and then places two electrodes into the solid to see if it conducts electricity. The electrodes are connected in series to a power pack and a lamp that will light if the lead fluoride conducts electricity. After making her first observation, the solid lead fluoride is heated strongly until it melts. The power pack is left switched on throughout the experiment. Describe and explain what the student will see. **[6]**

✎ *The quality of written communication will be assessed in your answer to this question.*

C5 Chemicals of the Natural Environment

The Earth's Resources

The Earth is made up of different parts.

The **atmosphere** is a layer of gas surrounding the Earth. It's made up of...
- the **elements** nitrogen, oxygen and argon
- some **compounds** (e.g. carbon dioxide and water vapour).

The **hydrosphere** is mostly made up of water and some dissolved compounds.

The **lithosphere** is the rigid outer layer of the Earth, made up of the crust and the part of the mantle just below it. It consists of a mixture of minerals (e.g. silicon dioxide), and an abundance of the elements silicon, oxygen and aluminium.

Chemicals of the Atmosphere

Dry atmospheric air is made from 78% nitrogen, 21% oxygen, nearly 1% argon and approximately 0.04% carbon dioxide.

The chemicals that make up the atmosphere consist of...
- non-metal elements
- molecular compounds made up from non-metal elements.

From the table below, you can see that the molecules (with the exception of water) that make up the atmosphere are gases at 20°C because they have low boiling points. This can be explained by looking at the structure of the molecules:
- Gases have small molecules **with weak forces of attraction between them**.
- Only small amounts of energy are needed to break these forces.

Pure molecular compounds don't conduct electricity because their molecules aren't charged.

(HT) The atoms within molecules are connected by strong **covalent bonds**. In a covalent bond...
- the **electrons** are shared between the **atoms**.
- a strong, **electrostatic attraction** is created between each positive nucleus and the shared pair of negative electrons.

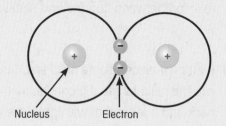

Nucleus   Electron

Chemical	2D Molecular Diagram	3D Molecular Diagram	Melting Point (°C)	Boiling Point (°C)
Oxygen, O_2	O=O		-218	-183
Nitrogen, N_2	N≡N		-210	-196
Carbon dioxide, CO_2	O=C=O		Sublimes (no liquid state)	-78
Water vapour, H_2O	H−O−H		0	100
Argon, Ar	Ar		-189	-186

Key Words   Atmosphere • Element • Compound • Hydrosphere • Lithosphere

Chemicals of the Natural Environment C5

Chemicals of the Lithosphere

The **lithosphere** is made from the crust and the part of the mantle just below it.

This table shows the abundance of some of the **elements** in the Earth's crust. For example, you can see that the three most abundant elements are…

- oxygen
- silicon
- aluminium.

N.B. You may be asked to interpret data like this in your exam.

Element	Abundance in Lithosphere (ppm)
Oxygen, O	455 000
Silicon, Si	272 000
Aluminium, Al	83 000
Iron, Fe	62 000
Calcium, Ca	46 600
Magnesium, Mg	27 640
Sodium, Na	22 700
Potassium, K	18 400
Titanium, Ti	6320
Hydrogen, H	1520
Carbon, C	940

Carbon in the Lithosphere

Diamond and **graphite** are both minerals formed from pure carbon that is found in the lithosphere.

You can see from the diagrams that in diamond, each carbon atom is covalently bonded to four other carbon atoms. This explains why diamond is very hard.

The diagram of graphite shows that each carbon atom is covalently bonded to three other carbon atoms and that they're arranged in sheets that can slide easily over each other. This explains why graphite is soft. Spare electrons can move between the layers of atoms, so graphite can conduct electricity.

In both graphite and diamond, the covalent bonds are strong, so they both have high melting points and are insoluble in water.

Structure of Diamond

Carbon atom →

← Strong covalent bond

Structure of Graphite

Carbon atom →

Strong covalent bond

Weak forces

Silicon Dioxide in the Lithosphere

A lot of the silicon and oxygen in the lithosphere is present as the compound silicon dioxide (SiO_2).

Silicon dioxide forms a giant covalent structure, so it has similar properties to diamond.

Silicon dioxide has the following properties:
- Hard
- High melting point
- Electrical insulator
- Insoluble in water.

C5 Chemicals of the Natural Environment

Chemicals of the Hydrosphere

Seawater in the **hydrosphere** is 'salty' because it contains dissolved **ionic compounds** called **salts**.

For example, sodium chloride is an ionic compound made from positive sodium **ions** and negative chloride ions. The ions are **electrostatically attracted** to each other to form a **giant 3D crystal lattice** with high melting and boiling points.

HT If given a table of charges on **ions**, you need to be able to work out the **formulae for salts** in the sea.

For example, you should be able to work out the formulae for sodium chloride, magnesium sulfate, potassium chloride and potassium bromide. This was covered in Module C4.

Properties of Ionic Compounds

Ionic compounds have similar properties: high melting points; they don't conduct electricity when solid; they do conduct electricity when molten or dissolved. Chemists developed an explanation of the structure of ionic compounds to explain these properties:

- They have high melting and boiling points because the ions are held together by strong forces of attraction in a lattice (see page 36).

- They don't conduct electricity when solid because the ions are fixed in place and can't move.
- They conduct electricity when molten (or dissolved) because the ions are free to move.

Many ionic compounds dissolve in water because the water molecules are polar (have a positive end and a negative end):

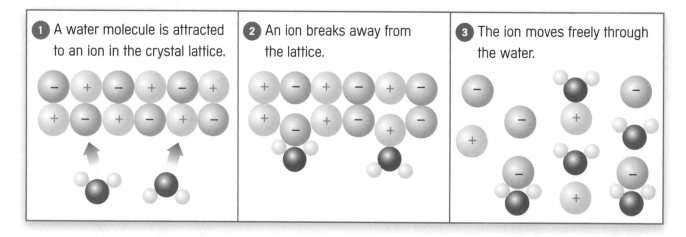

1 A water molecule is attracted to an ion in the crystal lattice.

2 An ion breaks away from the lattice.

3 The ion moves freely through the water.

Quick Test

1. What is meant by the term 'hydrosphere'?
2. What is the percentage of oxygen in dry air?
3. State two properties of diamond.
4. State two typical properties of ionic compounds.

Key Words   *Hydrosphere • Ionic compound • Ion*

Chemicals of the Natural Environment C5

Using Precipitation to Test for Ions

In the oceans calcium ions (Ca^{2+}) combine with carbonate ions (CO_3^{2-}) to form the **insoluble** ionic compound calcium carbonate ($CaCO_3$), or limestone. Insoluble solids formed in these types of reaction are called **precipitates**. We can use **precipitation** reactions to detect ions in aqueous solutions.

We can make predictions about precipitation reactions by interpreting information on solubility. For example, if we know that magnesium carbonate is insoluble, then mixing a solution that contains magnesium ions (e.g. magnesium chloride) with a solution that contains carbonate ions (e.g. sodium carbonate) will result in the precipitation of insoluble magnesium carbonate.

Testing for Metal Ions

Many positive metal ions can be identified in solution by adding sodium hydroxide solution (NaOH) and observing the colour of the precipitate.

You can see some of the results in the table. You don't need to learn the colours but you will be expected to interpret results tables in the exam.

Metal Ion Present	Colour of Precipitate When NaOH Added
Cu^{2+}	Light blue
Fe^{2+}	Green
Fe^{3+}	Red-brown

(HT) We know that the hydroxide ion has a single negative charge (OH^-). This means that we can work out the formula of the metal hydroxide produced and write a balanced ionic equation. Look at these examples:

$$Cu^{2+}(aq) + \cancel{2}OH^-(aq) \longrightarrow Cu(OH)_2(s)$$

$$Fe^{3+}(aq) + \cancel{3}OH^-(aq) \longrightarrow Fe(OH)_3(s)$$

You need two hydroxide ions to balance the charge on the Cu^{2+} ion, but three to balance the charge on the Fe^{3+} ion. Notice how this allows you to work out the formula of the metal hydroxide produced.

Testing for Negative Ions

Many negative (non-metal) ions can be identified in solution because they will react with other aqueous ions to produce an insoluble precipitate. Here are some examples:

Ion	Add	Observe	(HT) Ionic Equation
Chloride, Cl^-	$AgNO_3$(aq)	White precipitate	$Ag^+(aq) + Cl^-(aq) \longrightarrow AgCl(s)$
Bromide, Br^-	$AgNO_3$(aq)	Cream precipitate	$Ag^+(aq) + Br^-(aq) \longrightarrow AgBr(s)$
Iodide, I^-	$AgNO_3$(aq)	Yellow precipitate	$Ag^+(aq) + I^-(aq) \longrightarrow AgI(s)$
Sulfate, SO_4^{2-}	$Ba(NO_3)_2$(aq)	White precipitate	$Ba^{2+}(aq) + SO_4^{2-}(aq) \longrightarrow BaSO_4(s)$

C5 Chemicals of the Natural Environment

Extracting Useful Metals

Ores are rocks that contain varying amounts of **minerals**, from which **metals** can be extracted.

Sometimes very large amounts of ores need to be mined in order to recover a small percentage of valuable minerals, for example, copper.

The method of extraction depends on how reactive the metal is.

Metals that are less reactive than carbon (e.g. zinc, iron and copper) can be extracted from their oxides by heating with carbon:

- The metal oxide is **reduced**, as it has lost oxygen.
- The carbon is **oxidised**, as it has gained oxygen.

For example, zinc can be extracted from zinc oxide by heating it with carbon:

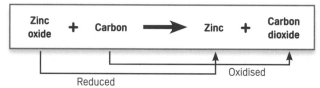

Relative Formula Mass

The **relative formula mass** (**RFM**) tells you the total mass of the atoms in a compound. All you have to do is add up the relative atomic masses (RAMs) that you can find on the periodic table. Here are two examples:

- The RFM of CO_2 is $12 + 16 + 16 = 44$
- The RFM of $CaCO_3$ is $40 + 12 + 16 + 16 + 16 = 100$
  (So in 100g of $CaCO_3$, 40g is calcium.)

$^{12}_{6}$**C** — Relative atomic mass of carbon is 12

$^{40}_{20}$**Ca** — Relative atomic mass of calcium is 40

$^{16}_{8}$**O** — Relative atomic mass of oxygen is 16

HT Calculating a Metal's Mass

If you're given its formula, you can calculate the mass of metal that can be extracted from a substance:

1. Write down the formula.
2. Work out the relative formula mass.
3. Work out the percentage mass of the metal.
4. Work out the mass of the metal.

Example

Find the mass of Zn that can be extracted from 100g of ZnO.

1. ZnO
2. Relative formula mass $= 65 + 16 = 81$
3. Percentage of zinc present

$$= \frac{\text{RAM of Zn}}{\text{RFM of ZnO}} \times 100 = \frac{65}{81} \times 100 = 80\%$$

4. In 100g of ZnO, there will be $\frac{80}{100} \times 100$

$$= \textbf{80g of Zn}$$

If you were given the equation of a reaction, you could find the ratio of the mass of the reactant to the mass of the product.

$$2ZnO_{(s)} + C_{(s)} \longrightarrow 2Zn_{(s)} + CO_{2(g)}$$

Relative formula mass:

Work out the RFM of each substance

$$(2 \times 81) + 12 = (2 \times 65) + 44$$
$$162 + 12 = 130 + 44$$
$$174 = 174$$

Therefore, 162g of ZnO produces 130g of Zn.

So, 1g of ZnO $= \frac{130}{162} = 0.8$g of Zn

and 100g of ZnO $= 0.8 \times 100 = \textbf{80g of Zn}$

Key Words   Ore • Relative formula mass

Electrolysis

Electrolysis is the breaking down of an **electrolyte** using an **electric current**.

The process is used to extract **reactive metals** from their ores because they're too reactive to be extracted by heating with carbon.

Ionic compounds conduct electricity when they're...
- molten
- dissolved in solution.

This is because their **ions** are free to move through the liquid.

When an ionic compound melts, electrostatic forces between the charged ions in the crystal lattice are broken down and the ions are free to move.

Electrolysis

Negative electrode —

Positive electrode +

When a direct current is passed through a molten ionic compound...
- positively charged ions are attracted towards the **negative electrode**
- negatively charged ions are attracted towards the **positive electrode**.

For example, in the electrolysis of molten lead bromide...
- positively charged lead ions are attracted towards the **negative electrode**, forming lead (a metal)
- negatively charged bromide ions are attracted towards the **positive electrode**, forming bromine (a non-metal).

HT When ions get to the oppositely charged electrode they're **discharged**, i.e. they lose their charge.

For example, in the electrolysis of molten lead bromide the non-metal ion loses electrons to the positive electrode to form a bromine atom. The bromine atom then bonds with a second atom to form a bromine molecule.

The reactions at the electrodes can be written as **half equations**. This means that you write separate equations for what is happening at each of the electrodes during electrolysis.

$$2Br^- \longrightarrow Br_2 + 2e^-$$

The lead ions gain electrons from the negative electrode to form a lead atom:

$$Pb^{2+} + 2e^- \longrightarrow Pb$$

This process completes the circuit as the electrons are exchanged at the electrodes.

C5 Chemicals of the Natural Environment

Extracting Aluminium by Electrolysis

Aluminium is extracted from its **ore** by **electrolysis**:

1. Aluminium ore (bauxite) is purified to leave aluminium oxide.
2. Aluminium oxide is mixed with cryolite (a compound of aluminium) to lower its melting point.
3. The mixture of aluminium oxide and cryolite is melted, so that the **ions** can move.
4. When a **current** passes through the molten mixture, positively charged aluminium ions move towards the **negative electrode**.
5. Aluminium is formed at the negative electrode.
6. Negatively charged oxide ions move towards the **positive electrode**.
7. Oxygen is formed at the positive electrode.

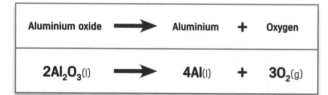

Aluminium oxide $\longrightarrow$	Aluminium	+	Oxygen
$2Al_2O_{3(l)} \longrightarrow$	$4Al_{(l)}$	+	$3O_{2(g)}$

HT At the negative electrode, aluminium ions gain electrons to become neutral atoms:

$$Al^{3+} + 3e^- \xrightarrow{\text{Reduction}} Al$$

At the positive electrode, oxygen ions lose electrons to become neutral atoms:

$$2O^{2-} - 4e^- \xrightarrow{\text{Oxidation}} O_2$$

This can also be written as:

$$2O^{2-} \longrightarrow O_2 + 4e^-$$

Metals and the Environment

This table shows the **environmental impacts** of extracting, using and disposing of metals.

A life cycle assessment helps scientists to make decisions about which method of extraction causes the least environmental damage.

Stage of Life Cycle	Process	Environmental Impact
Making the material from natural raw materials	Mining	• Lots of rock wasted. • Leaves a scar on the landscape. • Air / noise pollution.
	Processing	• Pollutants caused by transportation. • Energy usage. • Electrolysis uses more energy than reduction.
Manufacture	Manufacturing metal products	• Energy usage in processing and transportation.
Use	Transport to shops / home	• Pollutants caused by transportation.
	Running the product	• Energy usage.
Disposal	Reuse	• No impact.
	Recycle	• Uses a lot less energy than the initial manufacturing.
	Throw away	• Landfill sites remove wildlife habitats and are an eyesore.

Properties of Metals

A metal has a **giant structure** of **ions** that is held together by a strong force of attraction called the **metallic bond**. Metals...

- are **strong** – the ions are closely packed in a lattice structure
- have **high melting points** – a lot of energy is needed to break the strong metallic bonds.

(HT) Metals are also...

- **malleable** – they can be beaten into shape or dented as the layers of metal ions can slide over each other
- **conductors of electricity** – electrons are free to move throughout the structure. When a voltage is applied, the electrons move through the metal in one direction.

In a metal, the positively charged metal ions are held strongly together by a **'sea' of electrons**.

Lattice of positive ions

'Sea' of electrons that are all free to move

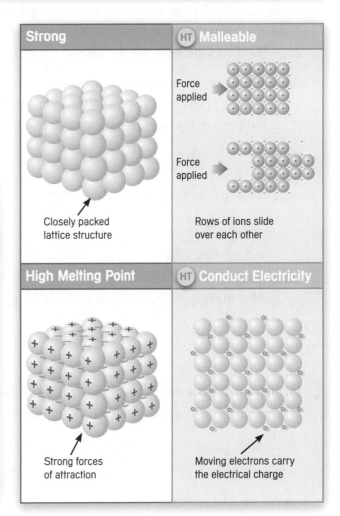

Strong	(HT) Malleable
Closely packed lattice structure	Force applied / Force applied — Rows of ions slide over each other
High Melting Point	(HT) **Conduct Electricity**
Strong forces of attraction	Moving electrons carry the electrical charge

Uses of Metals

The properties of metals determine how they're used:

- Titanium is **strong** and is used for replacement hip joints and submarines.
- Aluminium is **malleable** and is used for drinks cans.

- Iron has a **high melting point** and is used for making saucepans.
- Copper is an excellent **conductor** of electricity and is used for cables and electrical switches.

Quick Test

1. Describe how you would test for a metal ion in an aqueous solution.
2. Describe how you would test for the presence of sulfate ions.
3. What happens to the positive and negative ions in electrolysis?
4. Name the products at the positive and negative electrodes in the electrolysis of aluminium oxide.
5. (HT) Write a balanced ionic equation to show the formation of iron(III) hydroxide, $Fe(OH)_3$, from iron(III) ions (Fe^{3+}) and hydroxide ions (OH^-).

1 Waste water from a chemical factory must be processed to remove any ions that might cause pollution. Some ions are harmless but others are dangerous for plants and animals. The water from the chemical plant is regularly tested to ensure that it's safe to be released into the nearby river. The data sheet on page 96 shows the tests that are carried out to detect some of the ions in the water.

(a) Gemma is an analytical chemist working at the plant. She suspects that the water from the factory has been contaminated with copper(II) chloride. Describe two tests that she should carry out to confirm her hypothesis and state the results that she should expect to observe. **[4]**

....

....

....

....

(b) On another day, Gemma adds dilute hydrochloric acid to a water sample and observes bubbles. Identify the negative ion present in the water and name the gas produced. **[2]**

....

....

2 **(a)** Aluminium oxide powder is mixed with a substance called cryolite. The mixture is then melted. Describe what happens to the aluminium ions and the oxide ions when aluminium oxide melts. **[2]**

....

....

(b) The mixture of molten aluminium oxide and cryolite is then electrolysed. The diagram below shows this happening.

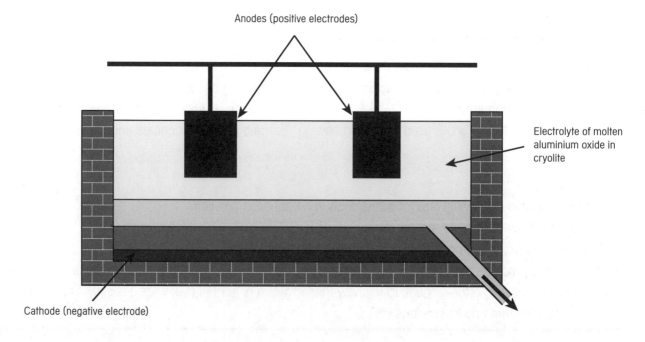

Anodes (positive electrodes)

Electrolyte of molten aluminium oxide in cryolite

Cathode (negative electrode)

Use the words provided to complete the following sentences. You can use words once, more than once, or not at all. **[2]**

nitrogen   **oxygen**   **bottom**   **top**   **aluminium**   **cathode**

Aluminium oxide breaks down into .... and aluminium when the current flows

through the molten aluminium oxide.

The aluminium metal forms at the .... of the cell, where it's siphoned off.

The .... gas is produced at the .... of the cell, at the

carbon anodes.

(c) Aluminium has several uses, including saucepans, power lines and aeroplanes. State which
properties of aluminium are important for each of these uses and use your understanding of
metallic bonding to explain why aluminium has these properties. **[6]**

✎ *The quality of written communication will be assessed in your answer to this question.*

....

....

....

....

....

....

....

....

HT **3** **(a)** Many metal ions can be detected in solution by precipitation. Zinc ions can be detected by adding
carbonate ions (CO_3^{2-}) to form the insoluble compound zinc carbonate ($ZnCO_3$). Work out the
charge on the zinc ion and then write a balanced ionic equation, including state symbols. **[3]**

....

....

(b) Copper ions (Cu^{2+}) can be detected using a solution of sodium hydroxide, which contains hydroxide
ions (OH^-). Write a balanced ionic equation, including state symbols, to show the formation of the
insoluble copper(II) hydroxide. **[3]**

....

C6 Chemical Synthesis

Chemicals

Chemical synthesis is the process by which raw materials are made into useful products including…
- food additives
- fertilisers
- dyestuffs
- pigments
- pharmaceuticals
- paints.

The chemical industry makes **bulk chemicals** on a very large scale and **fine chemicals** on a much smaller scale.

The range of chemicals made in industry and laboratories in the UK is illustrated in this pie chart:

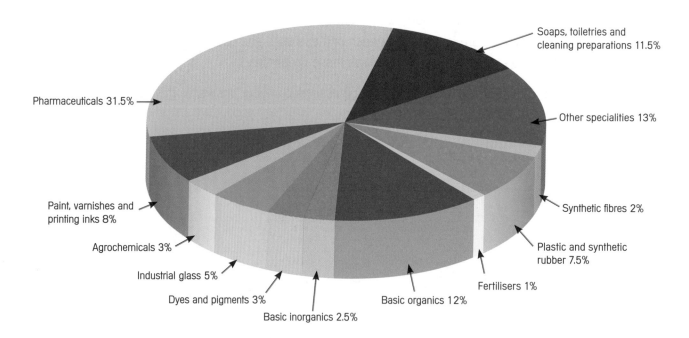

Soaps, toiletries and cleaning preparations 11.5%

Other specialities 13%

Synthetic fibres 2%

Plastic and synthetic rubber 7.5%

Fertilisers 1%

Basic organics 12%

Basic inorganics 2.5%

Dyes and pigments 3%

Industrial glass 5%

Agrochemicals 3%

Paint, varnishes and printing inks 8%

Pharmaceuticals 31.5%

Hazards

Many chemicals are **hazardous**, so it's important that you can…
- recognise the main hazard symbols
- understand the safety precautions to use.

Some examples of safety precautions are…
- wearing gloves and eye protection
- using safety screens
- not eating or drinking when working with chemicals
- not using flammable chemicals near to naked flames.

Corrosive

Explosive

Flammable

Oxidising

Harmful

Toxic

The pH Scale

The **pH scale** is a measure of the acidity or alkalinity of an **aqueous solution** across a 14-point scale:

- **Acids** are substances that have a pH less than 7.
- Bases are the oxides and hydroxides of metals. Soluble bases are called **alkalis** and have a pH greater than 7.

You can detect an acid or alkali using litmus paper.

You can measure the pH of a substance using an **indicator**, for example, universal indicator solution or a **pH meter**.

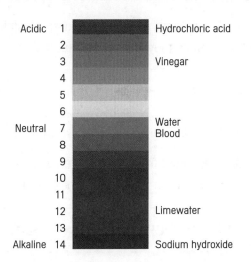

Acidic	1	Hydrochloric acid
	2	
	3	Vinegar
	4	
	5	
	6	
Neutral	7	Water / Blood
	8	
	9	
	10	
	11	
	12	Limewater
	13	
Alkaline	14	Sodium hydroxide

Acidic Compounds

Acidic compounds produce aqueous **hydrogen ions**, $H^+(aq)$, when they dissolve in water.

Common Acids	Formulae to Remember	State at Room Temp.
Citric acid	–	Solid
Tartaric acid	–	Solid
Nitric acid	HNO_3	Liquid
Sulfuric acid	H_2SO_4	Liquid
Ethanoic acid	–	Liquid
Hydrogen chloride (hydrochloric acid)	HCl	Gas (or aqueous)

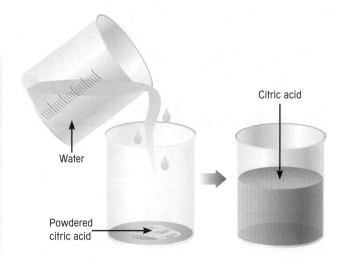

Water

Powdered citric acid

Citric acid

Alkali Compounds

Alkali compounds produce aqueous **hydroxide ions**, $OH^-(aq)$, when they dissolve in water.

Common Alkalis	Formulae to Remember
Sodium hydroxide	NaOH
Potassium hydroxide	–
Magnesium hydroxide	$Mg(OH)_2$
Calcium hydroxide	–

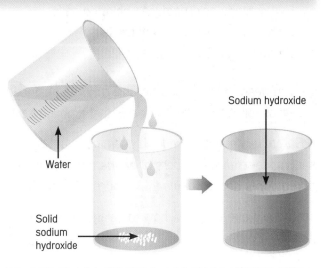

Water

Solid sodium hydroxide

Sodium hydroxide

C6 Chemical Synthesis

Neutralisation

When you mix together an **acid** and an **alkali** in the correct amounts they 'cancel out' each other.

Acid	+	Base	$\longrightarrow$	Salt	+	Water

This type of reaction is called **neutralisation**.

The **hydrogen ions** from the **acid** react with the **hydroxide ions** from the **alkali** to make water:

$$H^+\text{(aq)} + OH^-\text{(aq)} \longrightarrow H_2O\text{(l)}$$

For example, hydrochloric acid and potassium hydroxide can be neutralised:

Hydrochloric acid	+	Potassium hydroxide	$\longrightarrow$	Potassium chloride	+	Water
HCl(aq)	+	KOH(aq)	$\longrightarrow$	KCl(aq)	+	H_2O(l)

Neutralising Hydrochloric Acid (HCl) and Potassium Hydroxide (KOH)

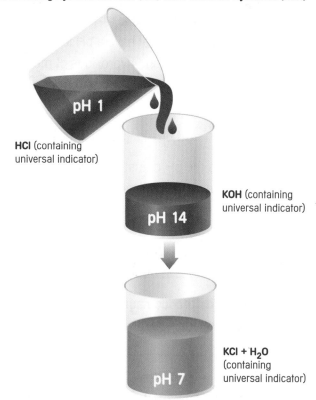

HCl (containing universal indicator)

pH 1

pH 14

KOH (containing universal indicator)

KCl + H₂O (containing universal indicator)

pH 7

Making Salts

Acids react with metal hydroxides, metal oxides and metal carbonates to form a salt and water. When an acid reacts with a metal carbonate, it also produces carbon dioxide.

Acids react with metals to form a salt and hydrogen.

The type of salt produced depends on the acid used:
- Hydro**chlor**ic acid produces **chloride** salts.
- **Sulf**uric acid produces **sulfate** salts.
- **Nitr**ic acid produces **nitrate** salts.

(HT) You need to know, and be able to write balanced equations for, the reactions of acids that produce salts.

*N.B. A balanced equation for a chemical reaction shows the relative numbers of **atoms** and molecules of **reactants** and **products** taking part in the reaction.*

You should already know how to balance equations that are unbalanced.

Hydrochloric acid	+	Sodium hydroxide	$\longrightarrow$	Sodium chloride	+	Water
HCl(aq)	+	$NaOH$(aq)	$\longrightarrow$	$NaCl$(aq)	+	H_2O(l)

Hydrochloric acid	+	Copper oxide	$\longrightarrow$	Copper chloride	+	Water
$2HCl$(aq)	+	CuO(s)	$\longrightarrow$	$CuCl_2$(aq)	+	H_2O(l)

Hydrochloric acid	+	Calcium carbonate	$\longrightarrow$	Calcium chloride	+	Water	+	Carbon dioxide
$2HCl$(aq)	+	$CaCO_3$(s)	$\longrightarrow$	$CaCl_2$(aq)	+	H_2O(l)	+	CO_2(g)

Hydrochloric acid	+	Magnesium	$\longrightarrow$	Magnesium chloride	+	Hydrogen
$2HCl$(aq)	+	Mg(s)	$\longrightarrow$	$MgCl_2$(aq)	+	H_2(g)

Formulae of Salts

You need to remember the formulae of the salts listed in this table:

Group	Salt	Formula
1	Sodium chloride	NaCl
1	Potassium chloride	KCl
1	Sodium carbonate	Na_2CO_3
1	Sodium nitrate	$NaNO_3$
1	Sodium sulfate	Na_2SO_4
2	Magnesium sulfate	$MgSO_4$
2	Magnesium carbonate	$MgCO_3$
2	Magnesium oxide	MgO
2	Magnesium chloride	$MgCl_2$
2	Calcium carbonate	$CaCO_3$
2	Calcium chloride	$CaCl_2$
2	Calcium sulfate	$CaSO_4$

Magnesium Sulfate Solution

HT You should already know how to write formulae for **ionic compounds**. Given the formulae of the salts listed in the table, you need to be able to work out the charge on each ion in a compound.

Energy Changes in Chemical Reactions

Exothermic changes (like combustion) release energy...
- usually as heat
- because the products have less energy than the reactants did.

Endothermic changes...
- are less common than exothermic changes
- take in energy, so usually feel cold to the touch. This means the products have more energy than the reactants did.

Endothermic reactions in industry can take a lot of energy to make them happen. Exothermic reactions can sometimes be dangerous because they can reach very high temperatures if they aren't adequately controlled.

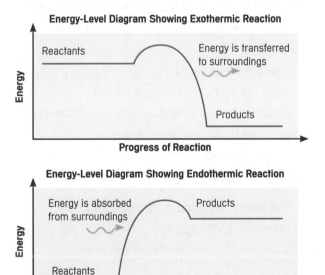

Energy-Level Diagram Showing Exothermic Reaction

Energy

Reactants

Energy is transferred to surroundings

Products

Progress of Reaction

Energy-Level Diagram Showing Endothermic Reaction

Energy

Energy is absorbed from surroundings

Products

Reactants

Progress of Reaction

Quick Test

1. Describe the hazard symbols for toxic and flammable.
2. State the formulae of hydrochloric acid and sulfuric acid.
3. What is the formula of sodium hydroxide?
4. HT Write a balanced symbol equation to show the reaction of magnesium oxide and nitric acid.

Key Words   **Exothermic • Endothermic**   53

C6 Chemical Synthesis

Percentage Yield

When chemical synthesis takes place, the starting materials (**reactants**) react to produce new substances (**products**). The greater the amount of reactants used, the greater the amount of product formed.

You can calculate the **percentage yield** by comparing...

- the actual yield – actual amount of product made
- the theoretical yield – amount of product you would expect to get if the reaction goes to completion.

$$\text{Percentage yield} = \frac{\text{Actual yield}}{\text{Theoretical yield}} \times 100$$

Chemical Synthesis

There are a number of different stages in any chemical synthesis of an inorganic compound:

1. Establish the **reaction** or series of reactions that are needed to make the **product**.
2. Carry out a risk assessment.

(HT) You need to work out the quantities of reactants to use.

3. Carry out the reaction under suitable conditions, e.g. temperature, concentration and use of a **catalyst**.
4. Separate the product from the reaction mixture.
5. **Purify** the product to ensure it's not contaminated by other products or **reactants**.
6. Weigh the mass and calculate the **percentage yield**.
7. Check the **yield** and **purity** by **titration**.

N.B. The purity of a product is important as impurities can be dangerous.

Ways of Purifying a Product

1. Filtration separates insoluble solids from dissolved substances.

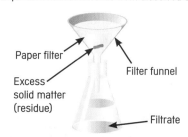

Paper filter

Filter funnel

Excess solid matter (residue)

Filtrate

2. Heating evaporates away the solvent (water) to leave behind crystals of the product. You can also make crystals by cooling the mixture.

Heat

3. Drying the product in a desiccator.

Checking the Purity

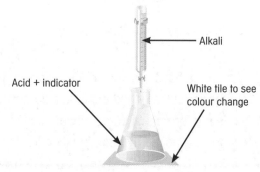

Alkali

Acid + indicator

White tile to see colour change

Relative Atomic Mass

The **relative atomic mass** (RAM) of an **element** shows the mass of one **atom** in comparison to the mass of other atoms.

You can obtain the relative atomic mass of an element by looking at the periodic table.

Examples are…

- RAM of Mg = 24
- RAM of Cu = 63.5
- RAM of C = 12
- RAM of K = 39.

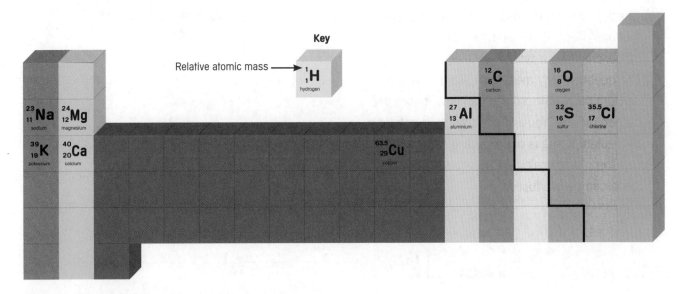

Relative Formula Mass

The **relative formula mass** (RFM or M_r) of a compound is the relative atomic masses of all its elements added together.

To calculate the RFM you need to know…
- the formula of the compound
- the RAM of each of the atoms involved.

Example

Calculate the RFM of water, H_2O.

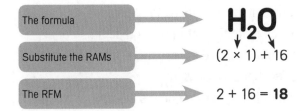

The formula	H_2O
Substitute the RAMs	$(2 \times 1) + 16$
The RFM	$2 + 16 = \mathbf{18}$

HT Quantity of Reactants

In chemical synthesis you need to work out how much of each reactant is required to make a known amount of product. To do this you need to know…
- how to find its relative atomic mass from the periodic table
- how to calculate its relative formula mass

- that a balanced equation shows the number of atoms or molecules of the reactants and products taking part in the reaction
- how to work out the ratio of the mass of reactants to the mass of products
- how to apply the ratio to the question.

C6 Chemical Synthesis

HT Finding the Mass of a Product

Example

Calculate how much calcium oxide can be produced from 50kg of calcium carbonate. (Relative atomic masses: Ca = 40, C = 12, O = 16).

1. Write down the equation.
2. Work out the RFM of each substance.
3. Check that the total mass of reactants equals the total mass of the products. If they aren't the same, check your work.
4. The question only mentions calcium oxide and calcium carbonate, so you can now ignore the carbon dioxide. You just need the ratio of mass of reactant to mass of product.
5. Use the ratio to calculate how much calcium oxide can be produced.

1
$$CaCO_3 \rightarrow CaO + CO_2$$

2
$$40 + 12 + (3 \times 16) \rightarrow (40 + 16) + [12 + (2 \times 16)]$$

3
$$100 \rightarrow 56 + 44 ✔$$

4
$$100 : 56$$

5
If 100kg of $CaCO_3$ produces 56kg of CaO,

then 1kg of $CaCO_3$ produces $\frac{56}{100}$ kg of CaO,

and 50kg of $CaCO_3$ produces $\frac{56}{100} \times 50$

$$= \textbf{28kg of CaO}$$

Finding the Mass of a Reactant

Example

Calculate how much aluminium oxide is needed to produce 540 tonnes of aluminium. (Relative atomic masses: Al = 27, O = 16).

1. Write down the equation.
2. Work out the RFM of each substance.
3. Check that the total mass of reactants equals the total mass of the products. If they aren't the same, check your work.
4. The question only mentions aluminium oxide and aluminium, so you can now ignore the oxygen. You just need the ratio of mass of reactant to mass of product.
5. Use the ratio to calculate how much aluminium oxide is needed.

1
$$2Al_2O_3 \rightarrow 4Al + 3O_2$$

2
$$2[(2 \times 27) + (3 \times 16)] \rightarrow (4 \times 27) + [3 \times (2 \times 16)]$$

3
$$204 \rightarrow 108 + 96 ✔$$

4
$$204 : 108$$

5
If 204 tonnes of Al_2O_3 produces 108 tonnes of Al,

then $\frac{204}{108}$ tonnes is needed to produce 1 tonne of Al,

and $\frac{204}{108} \times 540$ tonnes is needed to

produce 540 tonnes of Al

$$= \textbf{1020 tonnes of } Al_2O_3$$

Titration

Titration can be used to calculate the concentration of an **acid** by finding out how much **alkali** is needed to **neutralise** it.

Use this method:

1. Fill a burette with an alkali (of known concentration) and take an initial reading of the volume.
2. If you have been given a solid acid, accurately weigh out a sample of it and dissolve it in an accurately measured volume of distilled water.
3. Use a pipette to measure the aqueous acid into a conical flask. By using a pipette you will know the precise amount of acid used.
4. Now add a few drops of the indicator phenolphthalein (it should stay colourless).
5. Add alkali from the burette to the acid in the flask drop by drop.
6. Swirl the flask to mix it well. Near the end of the reaction, the indicator will start to turn pink. When the colour changes permanently, it means that the acid has been neutralised.

7. Record the volume of alkali added by subtracting the initial burette reading from the final burette reading.

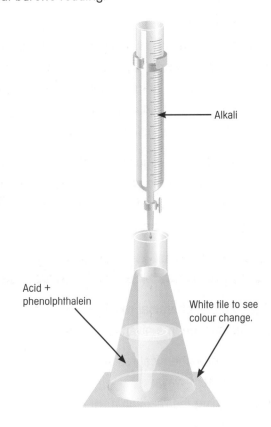

Alkali

Acid + phenolphthalein

White tile to see colour change.

Collecting Titration Data

In order to make sure that your titration result is a good estimate of the true value being measured, you'll need to repeat the titration. If one of the results is very different from the majority of the results, it could indicate that an error was made. This result should be repeated and perhaps ignored. Usually, when performing a titration, you repeat the experiment until you get two results that are the same.

Quick Test

1. What is the RFM of $MgCO_3$?
2. If the theoretical yield is 80kg but the actual yield is 60kg, what is the percentage yield?
3. Suggest three ways to purify a product.
4. How could you measure the yield and purity of a product?
5. HT What mass of CO_2 will be produced when 200kg of $CaCO_3$ is heated?
   The equation is $CaCO_3 \longrightarrow CaO + CO_2$

C6 Chemical Synthesis

Interpreting Titration Results

You may be asked to use a given formula to analyse some titration results.

Example

1.5g of impure citric acid was dissolved into 50cm^3 of water, and then sodium hydroxide (NaOH) was added from a burette until the acid was neutralised. The concentration of the sodium hydroxide solution was 20g/dm^3 and 34.4cm^3 was required to neutralise the citric acid in the conical flask.

Use the following equation to calculate the mass of pure citric acid in the sample. Use your answer to calculate the purity of the acid, as a percentage, using the equation provided.

$$\text{Mass of pure citric acid} = \frac{192 \times \text{Volume of NaOH} \times \text{Concentration of NaOH}}{120\,000}$$

So...

$$\text{Mass of pure citric acid} = \frac{192 \times 34.4 \times 20}{120\,000}$$

$$= \textbf{1.10g}$$

$$\text{Percentage purity} = \frac{\text{Actual mass of pure substance}}{\text{Mass of impure substance}} \times 100$$

So...

$$\text{Percentage purity} = \frac{1.10}{1.50} \times 100$$

$$= \textbf{73\%}$$

Rates of Reactions

The rate of a **chemical reaction** is the amount of products made in a given unit of time.

The rate of a chemical reaction can be found in three different ways:

1. Weighing the reaction mixture.
2. Measuring the volume of gas produced.
3. Observing the formation of a precipitate.

Weighing the reaction mixture – If one of the products is a gas, you could weigh the reaction mixture at timed intervals. The mass of the mixture will decrease as the gas is produced.

Measuring the volume of gas produced – You could use a gas syringe to measure the total volume of gas produced at timed intervals.

Observing the formation of a precipitate – This can be done by...

- watching a cross on a tile underneath the jar to see when it's no longer visible
- monitoring a colour change using a light sensor.

Weighing the Reaction Mixture

Measuring the Volume of Gas Produced

Observing the Formation of a Precipitate

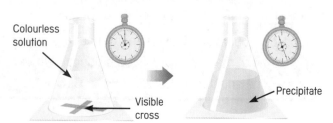

Colourless solution

Visible cross

Precipitate

Changing the Rate of Reaction

There are four important factors that speed up the rate of reaction:

1. Increasing the **temperature**.
2. Increasing the **concentration** of dissolved reactants.
3. Increasing the **surface area** by grinding lumps into powders.
4. Using a **catalyst**.

Collision Theory

It's easy to do experiments that show a correlation between increasing the concentration of a dissolved reactant and the rate of reaction.

However, a plausible scientific explanation of the link must also be found before the relationship can be considered to be an example of cause and effect.

Collision theory states that for two reactant particles to react, they must collide. But when they collide, they need to have enough energy so that they don't simply bounce off each other. This is called the **activation energy**.

If the reactant particles collide more **frequently**, the reaction will speed up. If the particles collide with more energy, they're more likely to have successful collisions, which will also speed up the reaction.

Concentration of Dissolved Reactants

In a **low concentration** reaction, there are fewer particles of **reactant** and the particles are more spread out. This means that the particles will collide less frequently.

In a **high concentration** reaction, there are more particles of reactant and the particles are crowded close together. This means that the particles will collide more frequently.

Low Concentration

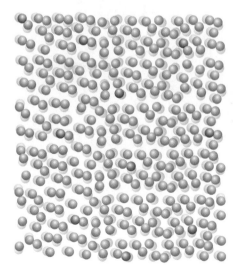

High Concentration

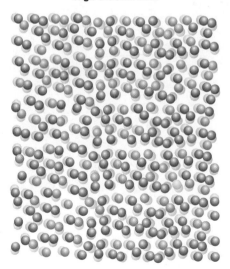

Key Water Reactant

C6 Chemical Synthesis

Surface Area of Solid Reactants

Large particles (for example, lumps of solid) have a **small surface area** in relation to their volume, which means that…

- fewer particles are exposed and available for collisions
- collisions are less frequent, so the reaction is slower.

Small particles (for example, powdered solids) have a **large surface area** in relation to their volume, which means that…

- more particles are exposed and available for collisions
- collisions are more frequent, so the reaction is faster.

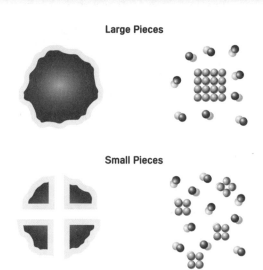

Large Pieces

Small Pieces

Using a Catalyst

Catalysts increase the rate of chemical reactions without being used up or changed during the process.

A catalyst…

- lowers the amount of energy needed for a successful collision
- makes more of the collisions successful
- speeds up the reaction.

Different reactions need different catalysts, for example…

- the production of ammonia uses an iron catalyst
- the production of sulfuric acid uses vanadium(V) oxide catalyst
- the production of nitric acid uses platinum / rhodium gauze catalyst.

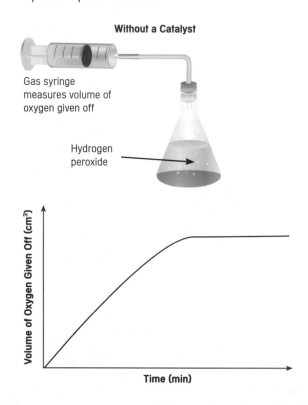

Without a Catalyst

Gas syringe measures volume of oxygen given off

Hydrogen peroxide

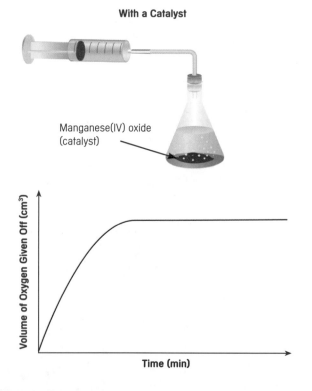

With a Catalyst

Manganese(IV) oxide (catalyst)

Analysing the Rate of Reaction

Graphs can be plotted to show the progress of a chemical reaction. There are three things you need to remember:

- The steeper the line, the faster the reaction.
- When one of the **reactants** is used up the reaction stops (line becomes flat).
- The same amount of **product** is formed from the same amount of **reactants**, irrespective of rate.

The graph shows that reaction A is faster than reaction B. This could be because…

- the surface area of the solid reactants in reaction A is greater than in reaction B
- the temperature of reaction A is greater than reaction B
- the concentration of the solution in reaction A is greater than in reaction B
- a catalyst is used in reaction A but not in reaction B.

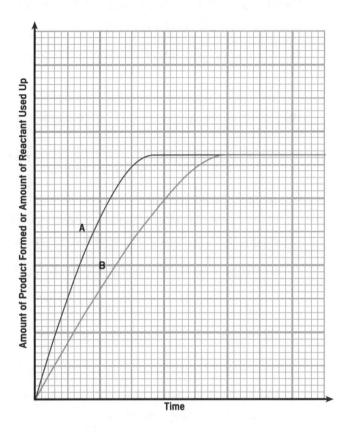

Controlling a Chemical Reaction

When carrying out a chemical synthesis on an industrial scale there are economic and safety factors to consider.

Examples of economic factors are as follows:

- The rate of manufacture must be high enough to produce a sufficient daily **yield** of product.
- Percentage yield must be high enough to produce a sufficient daily yield of product.
- A low percentage yield is acceptable providing the reaction can be repeated many times with recycled starting materials.
- Optimum conditions should be used that give the lowest cost rather than the fastest reaction or highest percentage yield.

Examples of safety factors are as follows:

- Care must be taken when using any reactants or products that could harm the environment if there was a leak.

- Care must be taken to avoid putting any harmful by-products into the environment.
- A risk assessment must be carried out, and the necessary precautions taken.

Quick Test

1. Define the term 'rate of reaction'.
2. List three ways to measure the rate of a reaction.
3. Why would chemists want to speed up the rate of an industrial reaction?
4. Explain why increasing the concentration speeds up a reaction.
5. Explain why powders react faster than lumps.
6. State three key points about a catalyst.

C6 Exam Practice Questions

1. Sherbet can be made by mixing three ingredients: sugar, citric acid and sodium hydrogencarbonate. When you put the sherbet in your mouth, the ingredients dissolve in your saliva and a neutralisation reaction occurs that produces a gas.

   (a) What would you expect the pH of a solution of citric acid to be? **[1]**

   ....

   (b) Complete the word equation for the reaction that occurs when sherbet dissolves in saliva. **[3]**

   .... + Sodium hydrogencarbonate ➡ Sodium citrate + ... + ...

   (c) Sometimes people suffer from acid indigestion, in which they have too much hydrochloric acid in their stomach. Martin suggests that this could be neutralised by swallowing tablets that contain magnesium, because he knows that magnesium reacts with acids to produce a neutral salt.

   (i) Write a word equation for the reaction between magnesium and hydrochloric acid. **[2]**

   ....

   (ii) Why is Martin's suggestion dangerous? **[1]**

   ....

   (iii) It's safer to treat acid indigestion using tablets that contain calcium carbonate or magnesium carbonate. Suggest why, using word equations to help explain your answer. **[3]**

   ....

   ....

   ....

   ....

2. Pam works for a company that manufactures fertilisers.

   (a) One of the fertilisers that she makes is ammonium nitrate. It's made from ammonium hydroxide (an alkali) and nitric acid.

   (i) Which ion is present in all acids? **[1]**

   ....

   (ii) Which ion is present in all alkalis? **[1]**

   ....

   (iii) Write an ionic equation, including state symbols, for the reaction between these two ions in a neutralisation reaction. **[2]**

   ....

   ....

(b) Pam makes a small quantity of ammonium nitrate, using a titration. Here are some of the steps that she follows. Fill in the empty boxes to put the steps in the correct order. Three have been done for you.   **[3]**

A Place some ammonium hydroxide into a conical flask and some nitric acid into a burette.

B Heat the solution to evaporate some of the water.

C Add two drops of indicator to the conical flask.

D Allow the solution to cool and crystals of ammonium nitrate to form.

E Add the nitric acid from the burette into the conical flask until the indicator changes colour.

F Dry the product in an oven or desiccator.

G Repeat the titration using the correct volume of acid and alkali but with no indicator.

| A | | | | | F | G |

HT **3** Gill investigates the reaction between magnesium carbonate and nitric acid, which produces magnesium nitrate, carbon dioxide and water. Here is a balanced symbol equation for this reaction:

$$MgCO_3 + 2HNO_3 \longrightarrow Mg(NO_3)_2 + H_2O + CO_2$$

Gill measures the rate of the reaction by measuring the amount of gas given off every 10 seconds. Here is a graph of her results:

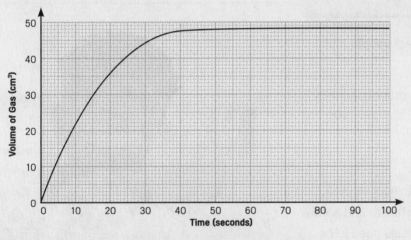

(a) What volume of gas was given off after 10 seconds?   **[1]**

(b) Suggest two ways that Gill could increase the rate of the reaction.   **[2]**

(c) Gill starts the reaction with 8.4g of magnesium carbonate. What mass of magnesium nitrate should she expect to produce?   **[3]**

C7 Further Chemistry

The Chemical Industry

The chemical industry synthesises chemicals on different scales according to their value.

Bulk chemicals are made on a large scale, e.g. …

- ammonia
- sulfuric acid
- sodium hydroxide
- phosphoric acid.

Fine chemicals are made on a small scale, e.g. …

- drugs
- food additives
- fragrances.

New chemical products or processes are the result of an extensive programme of research and development, for example, researching **catalysts** for new processes.

Health and Safety

Governments have a duty to protect **people** and the **environment**.

They impose **strict regulations** in order to control…
- chemical processes
- storage of chemicals
- transportation of chemicals.

In the UK, the Health and Safety Executive (HSE) is responsible for regulating risks to health and safety. For example, all hazardous chemicals need to be labelled with standard hazard symbols.

More recently, legislation has been passed to encourage companies to reduce the amount of pollution they produce.

Working in the Chemical Industry

You need to be able to interpret information about the work done by people who make chemicals. Chemists are required to…
- follow standard procedures
- carry out a titration
- scale up production
- interpret results
- carry out quality assurance.

Production of Chemicals

The production of useful chemicals involves several stages, including…

- preparation of feedstocks (starting materials)
- synthesis
- separation of products
- handling of by-products and waste
- monitoring purity.

Green Chemistry

Green chemistry is based on a number of principles that can lead to more **sustainable** processes. The sustainability of a chemical process depends on…

- the **atom economy**
- the use of **renewable** feedstocks
- energy inputs and outputs
- health and safety risks
- waste prevention
- the environmental impact
- social and economic benefits.

Atom economy is a measure of the amount of reactants that end up as useful products.

$$\text{Atom economy} = \frac{\text{Mass of atoms in the useful product}}{\text{Total mass of atoms in the reactants}} \times 100$$

The final product should aim to…

- contain all the **atoms** used in the process
- reduce waste products and increase **yield**.

The **percentage yield** of an experiment can be calculated using this formula:

$$\text{Percentage yield} = \frac{\text{Actual yield}}{\text{Theoretical yield}} \times 100$$

Renewable raw materials should be used whenever possible. Several companies are developing new materials from plants, but plants take up a lot of land. **Fertilisers** can be used to increase productivity but they use up a lot of energy during manufacture.

The energy needed to carry out a reaction should be minimised to reduce the environmental and economic impact. The processes should be carried out at ambient **temperature** and **pressure**.

C7 Further Chemistry

Green Chemistry (Cont.)

Substances used in a chemical process should be chosen to **minimise the risk** of chemical accidents.

Methods need to be developed to detect harmful products before they're made.

If waste isn't made, then it won't have to be cleaned up.

The **environmental impact** can be reduced by using alternatives to hazardous chemicals.

Efficient chemical products could be designed that...
- cause minimal harm to people or the environment
- are able to be broken down into non-toxic substances that don't stay in the environment.

Social benefits of green chemistry include...
- cleaner air quality
- cleaner buildings
- improved water quality in rivers and lakes.

Economic benefits include reduced energy costs.

Catalysts

In recent years there's been a lot of research and development into catalysts. Scientists share the results of their research at conferences and by publishing reports in peer reviewed journals. Before these reports are published, experts from the field evaluate the research.

Catalysts...
- reduce the activation energy needed for a reaction, so the process is faster and can take place at a lower temperature
- remain **unchanged** and can be used again and again, so the process is more sustainable.

Some industrial processes use enzyme catalysts. This may mean that the reaction needs to be done at an optimum pH and temperature (typically 37°C).

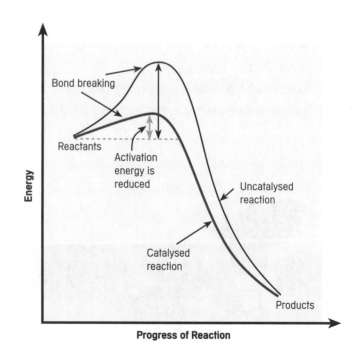

Alkanes and Alkenes

The **alkanes** are a group of **hydrocarbons**. In an alkane the carbon atoms are joined together by single carbon–carbon bonds.

Alkanes contain only single bonds, so they're **saturated** hydrocarbons.

Alkanes don't react with aqueous reagents because the C–C and C–H bonds are strong and unreactive. But they do burn well in plenty of air to produce…
- carbon dioxide
- water.

The table below shows the molecular and displayed formulae for the first four members of the alkane series. The general formula for an alkane is C_nH_{2n+2}, where n is the number of carbon atoms.

Another group of hydrocarbons is the **alkenes**. They have reactive C=C double bonds. They're described as **unsaturated**. The general formula for an alkene is C_nH_{2n}, where n is the number of carbon atoms.

HT You need to be able to write balanced symbol equations for the combustion of alkanes, for example:

$$CH_4(g) + 2O_2(g) \longrightarrow CO_2(g) + 2H_2O(g)$$

$$2C_4H_{10}(g) + 13O_2(g) \longrightarrow 8CO_2(g) + 10H_2O(g)$$

You should already know how to calculate masses of reactants and products from balanced equations (see page 56).

Alkane	Methane	Ethane	Propane	Butane
Molecular Formula	CH_4	C_2H_6	C_3H_8	C_4H_{10}
Displayed Formula	H H–C–H H	H H H–C–C–H H H	H H H H–C–C–C–H H H H	H H H H H–C–C–C–C–H H H H H

Alcohols

The characteristics of **alcohols** are due to the presence of the **functional group –OH**.

The general formula for alcohols is $C_nH_{2n+1}OH$, where n is the number of carbon atoms.

The two simplest alcohols are…
- methanol
- ethanol.

You must be able to recognise alcohols from their molecular and displayed formulae, and ball-and-stick diagrams of them.

Alcohol	Methanol	Ethanol
Molecular Formula	CH_3OH	C_2H_5OH
Displayed Formula	H H–C–O–H H	H H H–C–C–O–H H H

Key Words   Alkane • Hydrocarbon • Saturated • Alkene • Unsaturated

C7 Further Chemistry

Uses of Alcohols

Methanol can be used…
- as a chemical feedstock
- in the manufacture of cosmetics.

Ethanol can be used…
- as a solvent
- as a fuel.

Physical Properties of Alcohols

The properties of different alcohols can be explained by comparing their structures:
- Shorter alcohols have a low boiling point because the intermolecular forces are weak and don't need much energy to overcome them:

Methanol Molecule

- Longer hydrocarbons are less soluble in water because they behave more like an alkane, so they tend to float on top of water due to their low density:

Octanol Molecule

HT Reaction of Alcohols with Sodium

Alcohols react with sodium to produce a **salt** and **hydrogen gas**, for example:

Ethanol + Sodium → Sodium ethoxide + Hydrogen

$$2C_2H_5OH_{(l)} + 2Na_{(s)} \rightarrow 2C_2H_5O^-Na^+_{(s)} + H_{2(g)}$$

Alcohols, water and alkanes react differently with sodium:
- Sodium sinks in **alcohol**, doesn't melt and steadily gives off hydrogen.
- Sodium floats on **water**, melts, rushes around on the surface and rapidly gives off hydrogen.
- There is no reaction between sodium and an **alkane**.

Reaction of Alcohols with Air

Alcohols burn in air because of the presence of a hydrocarbon chain.

HT The following equation shows what happens when ethanol burns in air:

$$C_2H_5OH_{(l)} + 3O_{2(g)} \rightarrow 3H_2O_{(g)} + 2CO_{2(g)}$$

Quick Test

1. What is the name of the alkane with the formula C_4H_{10}?
2. What is the functional group present in all alcohols?
3. List one use for ethanol and one for methanol.
4. HT Write a balanced symbol equation for the complete combustion of butanol.

The Production of Ethanol

Ethanol can be produced by…
- synthesis
- **fermentation**
- biotechnology.

Ethanol is used on an industrial scale as a **feedstock**, **solvent** and **fuel**.

In your exam, you will need to be able to…
- interpret information about the processes used to produce ethanol
- evaluate the **sustainability** of the three processes
- appreciate that synthesis uses fossil fuels as a raw material, but using fermentation or biotechnology are more likely to be carbon neutral.

Synthesis

The following steps lead to the production of ethene, which can be used to produce ethanol:

1. Crude oil undergoes **fractional distillation**.
2. Long-chain **hydrocarbons** (**alkanes**) are vaporised and then cracked using a **catalyst** and heat.
3. The molecules are purified using fractional distillation.
4. The ethene that's produced can be used for a feedstock and the remaining water is removed.

Ethene is then reacted with steam at a high temperature and pressure in the presence of a catalyst to produce ethanol:

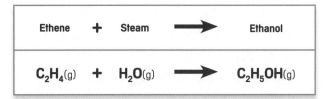

Ethene	+	Steam	→	Ethanol
$C_2H_4(g)$	+	$H_2O(g)$	→	$C_2H_5OH(g)$

Any unreacted products are recycled and fed through the system again.

Fermentation

Ethanol for use in alcoholic drinks (e.g. wine) is produced in the following way:

1. Water and yeast are mixed with natural sugars at just above room temperature.
2. **Enzymes** found in the yeast catalyse the formation of ethanol and carbon dioxide.
3. The carbon dioxide is allowed to escape from the reaction vessel, but air is prevented from entering it.

Glucose	→	Ethanol	+	Carbon dioxide
$C_6H_{12}O_6(aq)$	→	$2C_2H_5OH(aq)$	+	$2CO_2(g)$

C7 Further Chemistry

Fermentation (Cont.)

When ethanol solution is manufactured by fermentation, the concentration is limited by...

- the amount of sugar in the mixture
- the fact that, above a certain concentration, the ethanol kills the yeast.

When the fermentation reaction is over, the concentration of the ethanol may be increased by **distilling** the mixture.

This distillation process is used to produce spirits, for example...

- whisky
- brandy.

In some distilleries the whisky is distilled twice.

Optimum Fermentation Conditions

Optimum conditions are needed for the fermentation process:

- If the **temperature** is too high, the enzyme is denatured (the shape is irreversibly changed) and the reactant can no longer fit into the enzyme.
- If the pH changes too much, the enzyme is denatured.
- If oxygen is present, the ethanol is oxidised to form ethanoic acid (vinegar).

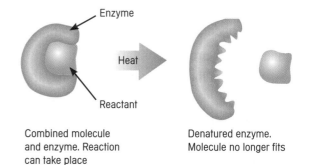

Combined molecule and enzyme. Reaction can take place

Denatured enzyme. Molecule no longer fits

Biotechnology

The biotechnology method produces ethanol using...

- genetically modified *E. coli* bacteria
- waste biomass.

The *E. coli* bacteria have had new genes introduced, which allow the bacteria to digest all the sugars in the biomass and convert them into ethanol.

This means that a wider range of biomass (for example, wood waste, corn stalks and rice hulls) can be converted to ethanol, rather than remaining as waste.

There are optimum conditions for this process:

- The temperature should remain 25–37°C.
- The optimum pH level needs to remain constant otherwise the enzyme will be **denatured**.

Bioethanol is Used as a Fuel

  Denatured enzyme

Carboxylic Acids

The characteristic properties of **carboxylic acids** are due to the presence of the **functional group −COOH**.

The two simplest carboxylic acids are…

* **methanoic acid**
* **ethanoic acid**.

Vinegar is a dilute solution of ethanoic acid.

You must be able to recognise carboxylic acids from their molecular and displayed formulae, and ball-and-stick diagrams of them.

Many carboxylic acids have unpleasant smells and tastes. For example, they're responsible for…

* the taste of vinegar
* the smell of sweaty socks
* the taste of rancid butter.

Carboxylic Acid	Methanoic acid	Ethanoic acid
Molecular Formula	HCOOH	CH_3COOH
Displayed Formula	$H-C{\overset{O}{\underset{O-H}{\diagup}}}$	$H-C{\overset{H}{\underset{H}{\mid}}}-C{\overset{O}{\underset{O-H}{\diagup}}}$

Chemical Reactions of Carboxylic Acids

Carboxylic acids are weak acids, which means they're less reactive than strong acids like sulfuric acid, nitric acid and hydrochloric acid. This also means that their pH values aren't as low as the values for strong acids.

Like all acids, they react with metals, carbonates and alkalis to produce acid salts.

Carboxylic acids react with…

* **metals** to form a salt and hydrogen
* **carbonates** to form a salt, water and carbon dioxide.

They can also be neutralised by **alkalis** to form a salt and water.

Examples

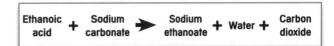

Esters

Carboxylic acids react with alcohols to form esters. This reaction is carried out in the presence of a **strong acid** catalyst.

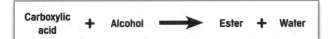

Esters…

* have **distinctive smells** that are responsible for the smells and flavours of fruits
* are used in the manufacture of perfumes and food products
* are also found in **solvents** and **plasticizers**.

C7 Further Chemistry

Fats

Fats and **oils** are naturally occurring esters. Living organisms make them to use as an energy store.

Fats are the esters of…
- **glycerol**
- **fatty acids**.

Saturated Fats

Animal fats (e.g. lard and fatty meat) are mostly **saturated molecules**:
- They have single carbon–carbon bonds (C–C).
- The molecules are unreactive.

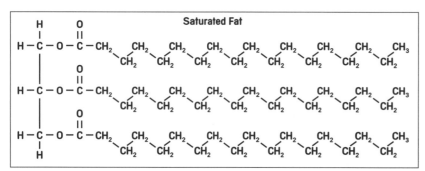

Unsaturated Fats

Vegetable oils (e.g. olive oil and sunflower oil) are mostly **unsaturated molecules**:
- They contain some double carbon–carbon bonds (C=C).
- The molecules are more reactive.

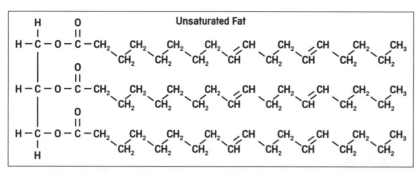

Quick Test

1. Give three ways that ethanol could be produced.
2. What happens to enzymes if they get too hot?
3. What functional group is present in carboxylic acids?
4. What sort of chemical do you think might be used as the flavouring in pear drops?

HT Method for Preparing Esters

1 Ethanol and excess ethanoic acid are heated under **reflux** in the presence of concentrated sulfuric acid. Reflux is a process of continual **evaporation** and **condensation**, i.e. the mixture is continually heated and returned to the flask.

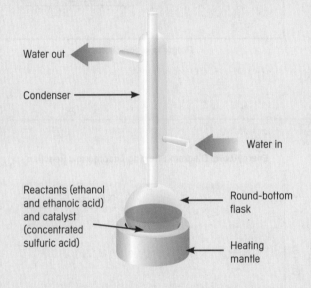

Water out

Condenser

Water in

Reactants (ethanol and ethanoic acid) and catalyst (concentrated sulfuric acid)

Round-bottom flask

Heating mantle

2 The **ester** is removed by **distillation**. (Ethyl ethanoate boils at 77°C.) In the distillation process, the liquid that has turned into a gas is removed from the reacting mixture.

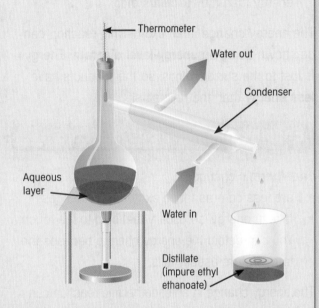

Thermometer

Water out

Condenser

Aqueous layer

Water in

Distillate (impure ethyl ethanoate)

3 The **distillate** is transferred to a separating funnel where it's **purified**:

- A solution of sodium carbonate is added, and the mixture is shaken.
- This mixture will react with any remaining acid and extract it into the aqueous phase.
- The aqueous phase is then run off.

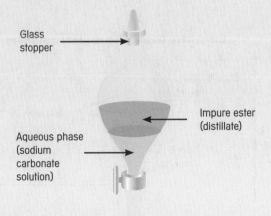

Glass stopper

Impure ester (distillate)

Aqueous phase (sodium carbonate solution)

4 The product is transferred to a conical flask and anhydrous calcium chloride is added to remove any remaining water molecules. The calcium chloride is removed later by **filtration**.

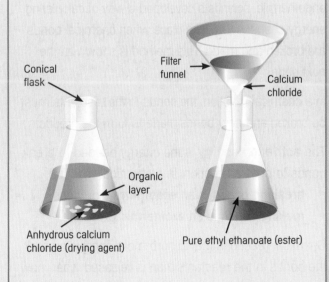

Conical flask

Filter funnel

Calcium chloride

Organic layer

Anhydrous calcium chloride (drying agent)

Pure ethyl ethanoate (ester)

C7 Further Chemistry

Exothermic Reactions

Exothermic changes (like combustion)…

- release energy, usually as heat, and you can detect this energy because there is usually a temperature rise
- release energy because the **products** have less energy than the **reactants** did.

The energy change in an exothermic reaction can be shown using an **energy-level diagram**. Energy is lost to the surroundings, so the products have **less energy** than the reactants.

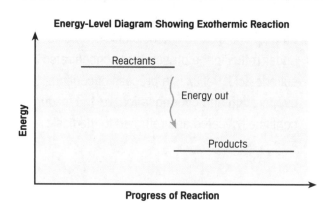

Energy-Level Diagram Showing Exothermic Reaction

Endothermic Reactions

Endothermic changes…

- are less common than exothermic changes
- take in energy, so usually feel cold to the touch. You can detect the energy change because the temperature usually falls.

The energy change in an endothermic reaction can be shown using an energy-level diagram. Energy is taken in from the surroundings during the reaction, so the products have **more energy** than the reactants.

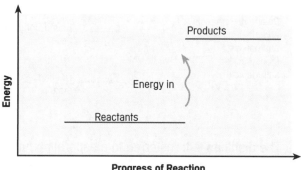

Energy-Level Diagram Showing Endothermic Reaction

Making and Breaking Bonds

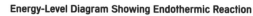

In order to explain why a reaction is exothermic or endothermic, scientists developed a way of calculating energy changes that take place when chemical bonds are broken and made. This method is shown on the next page.

In a chemical reaction, the bonds in the reactants must be broken and new bonds made to form the products.

The **activation energy** is the energy needed to break bonds to start a reaction. In a chemical reaction…

- **breaking** bonds is an **endothermic** process
- **making** bonds is an **exothermic** process.

Chemical reactions that absorb more energy to break the bonds in the reactants than is released when new bonds are made in the products, are **endothermic**.

Chemical reactions in which more energy is released when new bonds are made than was absorbed to break the old bonds, are **exothermic**.

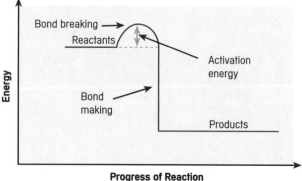

Energy-Level Diagram Showing Activation Energy

Key Words   Exothermic • Product • Reactant • Endothermic • Activation energy

HT Energy Calculations – Example 1

Hydrogen is burned in oxygen to produce water:

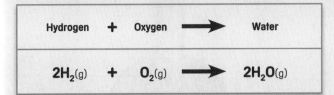

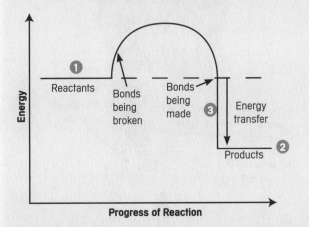

The following are **bond energies** for the **reactants** and **products**:

H–H is 436kJ   O=O is 496kJ   O–H is 463kJ

You can calculate the energy change using this method:

1. Calculate the energy used to break bonds:
   (2 × H–H) + O=O = (2 × 436) + 496 = **1368kJ**
2. Calculate the energy released when new bonds are made:
   (Water is made up of 2 × O–H bonds)
   2 × H–O–H = 2 × (2 × 463) = **1852kJ**
3. Energy change (ΔH) = nergy used to break bonds – Energy released when new bonds are made:
   = 1368 – 1852 = **-484kJ**

The reaction is **exothermic** because the energy from making the bonds is **more than** the energy needed to break the bonds.

Energy Calculations – Example 2

Hydrogen and halogens react together to form hydrogen halides. For example, the formation of hydrogen chloride is as follows:

Hydrogen	**+**	Chlorine	⟶	Hydrogen chloride
$H_2(g)$	**+**	$Cl_2(g)$	⟶	$2HCl(g)$

The following are bond energies for the reactants and products:

H–H is 436kJ   Cl–Cl is 243kJ   H–Cl is 432kJ

You can calculate the energy change as follows:

1. Calculate the energy used to break bonds:
   H–H + Cl–Cl = 436 + 243 = **679kJ**
2. Calculate the energy released when new bonds are made:
   2 × H–Cl = 2 × 432 = **864kJ**
3. Energy change (ΔH) = Energy used to break bonds – Energy released when new bonds are made:
   = 679 – 864 = **-185kJ**

The reaction is **exothermic**.

Quick Test

1. What type of reaction takes in energy from its surroundings?
2. Is making bonds endothermic or exothermic?
3. If a reaction takes in more energy to break the reactants' bonds than it releases when the products are made, will it be endothermic or exothermic?
4. HT In the purification of an ester, why is sodium carbonate added to the separating funnel?

C7 Further Chemistry

Reversible Reactions

Some chemical reactions are **reversible**. In a reversible reaction, the **products** can react together to produce the original **reactants**. We represent this with a special double-headed arrow: $\rightleftharpoons$

$$A \; + \; B \; \rightleftharpoons \; C \; + \; D$$

This means that...

- A and B can react together to produce C and D
- C and D can react together to produce A and B.

For example, the decomposition of ammonium chloride is a reversible reaction:

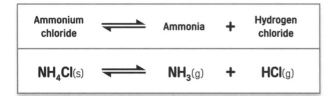

Ammonium chloride	$\rightleftharpoons$	Ammonia	+	Hydrogen chloride
$NH_4Cl_{(s)}$	$\rightleftharpoons$	$NH_{3(g)}$	+	$HCl_{(g)}$

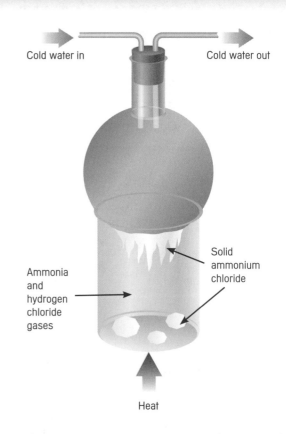

Cold water in

Cold water out

Solid ammonium chloride

Ammonia and hydrogen chloride gases

Heat

Dynamic Equilibrium

A reversible reaction will reach a state of **dynamic equilibrium** if it's in a closed system and left for long enough.

At equilibrium, the concentration of reactants and products doesn't change over time. The relative amounts of all the reacting substances at equilibrium depend on the conditions of the reaction.

HT When a dynamic equilibrium is established, the forward and backward reactions happen at exactly the same rate, which explains why the concentration of products (and reactants) doesn't change over time. You can think of this as like the number of people in a department store with a revolving door. As long as one person enters when one person leaves, there's a constant number of people in the store – a steady state.

The Importance of Nitrogen Fixation

Nitrogen is needed by plants in the form of nitrate ions, but they can't extract nitrogen from the air. Some bacteria can 'fix' nitrogen from the air and convert it to nitrates using enzymes as catalysts. However, natural nitrogen-fixing processes aren't sufficient to produce enough nitrates to grow sufficient food to feed the world's population.

Synthetic Fertilisers Can Help to Meet the Worldwide Demand for Food

The Haber Process

The Haber process converts atmospheric nitrogen to ammonia by reacting it with hydrogen from natural gas.

$$N_2(g) + 3H_2(g) \rightleftharpoons 2NH_3(g)$$

Ammonia is used to make fertilisers, explosives, dyes, medicines and a variety of other essential chemicals.

As the reaction is reversible, only a small amount of the gas (typically 15–30%) leaving the reactor is ammonia. Unreacted nitrogen and hydrogen are recycled to improve the **yield**. This is more cost effective than leaving the reaction for long enough for it to reach **dynamic equilibrium**.

Haber Process

Typical reactor conditions:
- iron catalyst
- 200 atmospheres pressure
- 450°C temperature

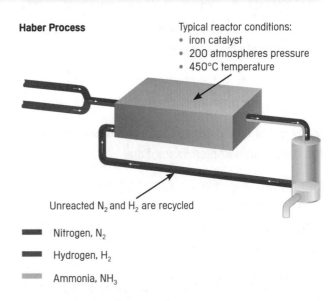

Unreacted N_2 and H_2 are recycled

Nitrogen, N_2

Hydrogen, H_2

Ammonia, NH_3

The Economics of the Haber Process

Controlled experiments (**fair tests**), in which only one variable was changed, generated the data shown on each of the three lines in the graph below. The pressure was changed while the temperature was maintained at 350°C to produce the top line. Then the pressure was changed while the temperature was maintained at 450°C to produce the middle line, and so on.

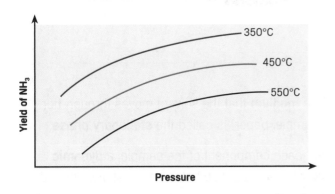

To increase the rate of the reaction, scientists are always looking for new catalysts. They hope to find catalysts that mimic natural enzymes to avoid the need for high temperatures and pressures, which are expensive and have a large carbon footprint.

(HT) Increasing the pressure increases the yield but the stronger equipment needed is expensive and so are the running costs. Safety may also be an issue at very high pressures. The pressure used is a compromise between cost and yield.

Increasing the temperature reduces the yield but increases the reaction rate. The temperature chosen is a compromise between rate and yield. The catalyst helps to speed up the reaction as well, but it doesn't affect the yield.

Quick Test

1. What does the $\rightleftharpoons$ symbol mean?
2. What are the raw materials for the Haber process and where do they come from?
3. Why are the unreacted gases leaving the Haber process reactor recycled?

C7 Further Chemistry

Analysis

Qualitative analysis is any method used to identify the **chemicals** in a substance.

Quantitative analysis is any method used to determine the **amount** of chemical in a substance.

Many of the analytical methods you have learned are based on samples in solutions.

When collecting data, it's important that the samples are representative of the **bulk** of the material under test. This is achieved by collecting multiple samples at **random**.

Analytical Procedures

There are **standard procedures** for the collection, storage and preparation of samples for analysis. After a sample has been collected, it should be stored in a **clean and sterile container** to prevent change, contamination or deterioration. The container should be…

- sealed
- labelled
- stored in a safe place.

Using a system of common practices and procedures can increase **reliability** since there's less room for human error.

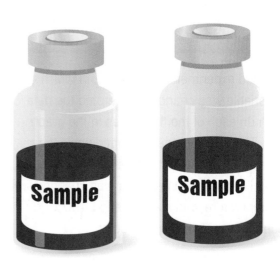

Chromatography

Chromatography is used to find out what unknown mixtures are made up of.

Substances are **separated** as they move through the **stationary phase** at different speeds, while dissolved in the **mobile phase**.

The **solvent** that's used to move the solution is called the **mobile phase**. Solvents can be…

- **aqueous** – water based
- **non-aqueous** – made from organic liquids such as **alkanes**.

The **medium** that the solvent moves through (for example, paper) is called the **stationary phase**.

For each component of the sample, a **dynamic equilibrium** is set up between the stationary and mobile phase.

The overall separation depends on the distribution of the compounds in the sample between the mobile and stationary phases.

Key Words Qualitative analysis • Quantitative analysis • Chromatography • Solvent • Alkane

Paper Chromatography

Paper chromatography has five main stages:

1. If the substance to be analysed is a solid, dissolve it in a suitable **solvent**.
2. Place a spot of the resulting solution onto a sheet of chromatography paper on the pencil line and allow it to dry.
3. Place the bottom edge of the paper into a suitable solvent.
4. As the solvent rises up the paper, it dissolves the 'spot' and carries it up the paper.
5. The different chemicals in the mixture separate because their molecules have different sizes and properties.

Stationary phase (paper)

Level reached by solvent

Three substances have been separated from the original mixture

Original spot

Pencil line

Mobile phase (solvent)

Thin Layer Chromatography

Thin layer chromatography (TLC) is similar to paper chromatography but the stationary phase is a thin layer of absorbent material (e.g. silica gel), supported on a flat, unreactive surface (e.g. a glass plate).

There are several advantages of TLC over paper chromatography.

Advantages of TLC include...

- faster runs
- more even movement of the mobile phase through the stationary phase
- a choice of different absorbencies for the stationary phase.

As a result, TLC usually produces better separations for a wider range of substances.

Chromatograms

A chromatogram is formed when the chemicals come out of solution and bind to the stationary phase. The chromatogram can then be compared to standard chromatograms (**standard reference materials**) of known substances to identify the different chemicals.

Some chromatograms have to be developed using **locating agents** to show the presence of colourless substances:

- Colourless spots can sometimes be viewed under ultraviolet (UV) light and then marked on the plate.
- The chromatogram can be viewed by being sprayed with a chemical that reacts with the spots to cause coloration.

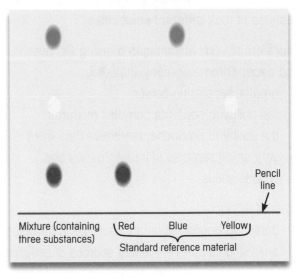

Paper Chromatogram

Pencil line

Mixture (containing three substances) | Red | Blue | Yellow

Standard reference material

C7 Further Chemistry

R$_f$ Value

The movement of a substance relative to the movement of the solvent front is known as the **R$_f$ value**.

You can work out the R$_f$ value using this formula:

$$R_f \text{ value} = \frac{\text{Distance travelled by substance}}{\text{Distance travelled by solvent}}$$

Calculating the R$_f$ value can help identify unknown substances.

The calculated R$_f$ value can be compared to known values for different substances.

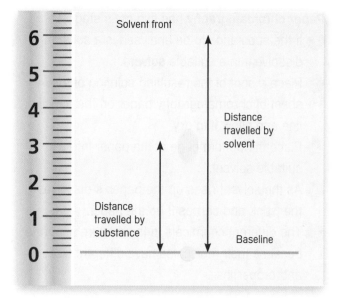

Gas Chromatography

In **gas chromatography** (GC)...
- the **mobile phase** is a carrier gas
- the **stationary phase** is a microscopic layer of liquid on an unreactive solid support
- the liquid is inside glass or metal tubing, called a **column**.

A sample of the substance to be analysed is injected into one end of the heated column, where it **vaporises**. The carrier gas then carries it through the column, where separation takes place.

GC is able to separate the components in a mixture because of their **different solubilities**.

There are several advantages of using GC over TLC and paper chromatography, including...
- greater separating power
- the ability to separate complex mixtures
- the ability to produce quantitative data from very small samples of liquids, gases and volatile solids.

Uses of GC include...
- detecting banned substances in blood samples
- analysing oil spills to identify sources of pollution.

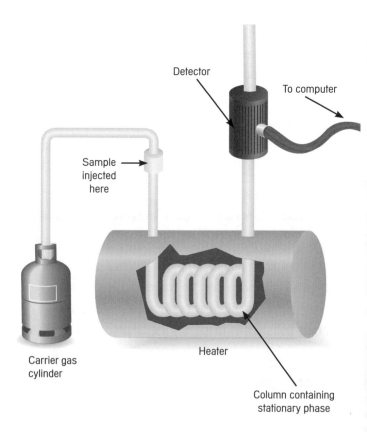

GC Analysis

The size of each peak in a gas **chromatogram** shows the relative amount of each chemical in the sample.

For example, this chart shows six different **compounds** present in a sample. The chart shows that…

- Compound A is present in the largest amount
- Compound D is present in the smallest amount.

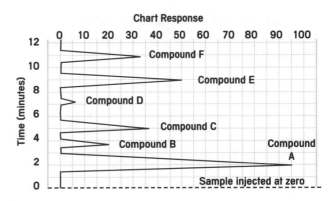

Retention Time

The **retention time** is the time taken for each substance to pass through the chromatographic system.

In GC, the retention time is the time taken from the substance being injected into the system to when the substance is detected.

Tables of relative retention times show the retention times of different chemicals relative to the retention time of a specific compound.

For example, this table shows that Compound B could be methanol because the retention times are the same:

Compound	Retention Time (minutes)
Methanol	2.24
A	2.08
B	2.24
C	3.01

Quantitative Analysis

There are six main stages of a **quantitative analysis**:

1. Choose an analytical method and take a sample that represents the bulk material.
2. Accurately measure out the sample.
3. Dissolve the sample (if it's a solid), taking care not to lose any of the sample in the process.
4. Measure a property of a solution that's proportional to the amount of chemical in the sample.
5. Calculate a value from the measurements.
6. Estimate the uncertainty of your results:
   - Compare values from repeat samples to find the range.
   - Work out the average value.
   - State how confident you are about the results.

Quick Test

1. Why is it important to test several samples when analysing a substance?
2. In paper chromatography, what are the mobile and stationary phases?
3. How is the R_f value calculated?
4. In gas chromatography, what is the 'retention time'?

C7 Further Chemistry

Standard Solutions

The concentrations of **standard solutions** are known accurately, so they can be used to measure the concentration of other solutions. The **concentration** of a solution is measured in g/dm^3.

The following procedure is used to make up a standard solution:

1. Weigh out 5g of solid sample in a beaker.
2. Transfer the solid sample into a volumetric flask, using a short-stem funnel. Wash the funnel and beaker with **distilled water**. Pour the washings into the volumetric flask to make sure that all the solid has been transferred.
3. Add distilled water to the flask until it's about three-quarters full. Place the stopper in the top and gently shake until all the solid is dissolved.
4. Place the flask on a level surface and fill with water until the level of solution reaches the $100cm^3$ mark.
5. Invert the flask to mix the contents and ensure an even concentration throughout.

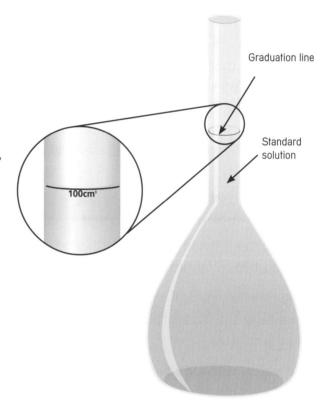

Graduation line

Standard solution

$100cm^3$

HT Calculating Concentration and Mass

You can calculate the concentration of a solution using this formula:

$$\text{Concentration (g/dm}^3) = \frac{\text{Mass (g)}}{\text{Volume (dm}^3)}$$

Example

Calculate the concentration of the solution when 3.6g of copper sulfate is dissolved in $80cm^3$ of water.

First, convert cm^3 to dm^3 by dividing by 1000.

$$\frac{80}{1000} = 0.08dm^3$$

Then calculate the concentration.

$$\text{Concentration} = \frac{\text{Mass}}{\text{Volume}}$$

$$= \frac{3.6g}{0.08dm^3} = \textbf{45g/dm}^3$$

You can work out the mass of solute by rearranging the concentration formula.

Example

Calculate the mass of solute if the concentration of a solution is $42g/dm^3$ and the volume is $2dm^3$.

Mass = Concentration × Volume

Mass = 42 × 2 = **84g**

Titration

Acid–alkali titration is an important method of quantitative analysis.

Use the following method:

1. Fill a **burette** with the **alkali** (of known concentration) and take a reading of the volume.
2. Accurately weigh out a 4g sample of solid **acid** and dissolve it in 100cm³ of distilled water.
3. Use a **pipette** to measure 25cm³ of the aqueous acid and put it into a conical flask. Add a few drops of an indicator (e.g. phenolphthalein) to the conical flask. (The indicator will show its acidic colour.) Place the flask on a white tile under the burette.
4. Add the alkali from the burette to the acid in the flask drop by drop. Swirl the flask to mix it well. Near the end of the reaction, the indicator will start to show the alkali colour (e.g. pink for phenolphthalein). When the colour changes permanently, it means the acid has been **neutralised**.
5. Record the volume of the alkali added by subtracting the amount in the burette at the end of the reaction from the starting value.
6. Repeat the whole procedure until you get two results that are the same, or repeat three times and take the average.

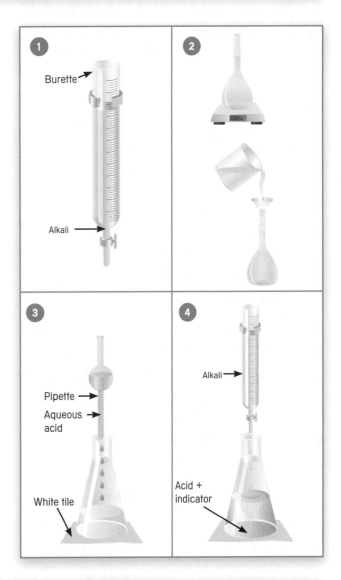

Measuring pH

As well as an indicator, a **pH probe** can be used to measure the change in pH. A **pH/volume graph** can be used to show how much alkali has been added to neutralise the acid.

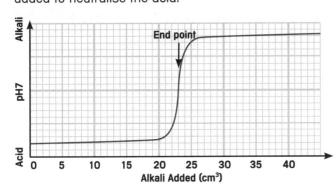

From a pH/volume graph, you can find…
- the volume of alkali added
- the end point of the reaction (i.e. where a rapid change in pH occurs).

This volume can be used in titration calculations to work out unknown concentrations.

C7 Further Chemistry

Interpreting Titration Results

You need to be able to use an equation that you're given to calculate the concentration of an acid or alkali.

Example

Calculate the concentration of hydrochloric acid when...

- concentration of sodium hydroxide (NaOH) = $30g/dm^3$
- volume of sodium hydroxide = $25cm^3$
- volume of hydrochloric acid added:
  - Experiment 1: $10.0cm^3$
  - Experiment 2: $9.9cm^3$
  - Experiment 3: $10.1cm^3$

First, work out the average volume of hydrochloric acid used in the three experiments.

$$\text{Average volume} = \frac{10.0cm^3 + 9.9cm^3 + 10.1cm^3}{3}$$

$$= 10cm^3$$

Then, using the titration formula below, calculate the concentration of hydrochloric acid.

$$\text{Concentration of acid } (g/dm^3) = \frac{\text{Volume of NaOH } (dm^3) \times \text{Concentration of NaOH } (g/dm^3) \times 0.9125}{\text{Volume of acid } (dm^3)}$$

You must work in dm^3 when doing calculations. To convert cm^3 to dm^3 divide by 1000.

$$\text{Concentration of hydrochloric acid} = \frac{\left(\frac{25cm^3}{1000}\right) \times 30g/dm^3 \times 0.9125}{\left(\frac{10cm^3}{1000}\right)}$$

$$= \textbf{68g/dm}^3 \text{ (answer rounded to nearest } g/dm^3)$$

HT You need to be able to interpret the results of a titration using a balanced equation and the **relative formula masses**.

Example

A titration is carried out and $35cm^3$ of sulfuric acid of concentration $60g/dm^3$ neutralises $25cm^3$ of sodium hydroxide. Calculate the concentration of sodium hydroxide.

1 Work out the relative formula mass of the acid and alkali.

$$H_2SO_4 = 2 + 32 + (4 \times 16) = 98$$
$$NaOH = 23 + 16 + 1 = 40$$

2 Write down the equation.

$$H_2SO_4(aq) + 2NaOH(aq) = Na_2SO_4(aq) + 2H_2O(l)$$
$$\textbf{98} \qquad\qquad \textbf{2 × 40}$$

This means that 98g of sulfuric acid reacts with 80g of sodium hydroxide.

3 Work out the mass of sulfuric acid used in the titration.

$$\text{Mass} = \text{Concentration} \times \text{Volume}$$
$$= 60g/dm^3 \times \left(\frac{35cm^3}{1000}\right)$$
$$= 2.1g$$

4 Work out the mass of sodium hydroxide used in the reaction.

If 98g of sulfuric acid reacts with 80g of sodium hydroxide, then 2.1g reacts with

$$\frac{2.1}{98} \times 80g = 1.7g \text{ sodium hydroxide.}$$

5 Work out the concentration of sodium hydroxide.

$$\text{Concentration} = \frac{\text{Mass}}{\text{Volume}}$$

$$= \frac{1.7}{\left(\frac{25cm^3}{1000}\right)}$$

$$= \textbf{68g/dm}^3$$

Evaluating Experimental Results

The **validity** of an experiment can depend on the **accuracy** of the results. Inaccurate results can be the result of errors of measurement or mistakes.

Mistakes can include…
- misreading a scale
- forgetting to fill up a burette to the correct level
- taking a thermometer out of the solution to read the scale.

Accuracy describes how close a result is to the 'actual' value.

Precision is a measure of the spread of the measured values. A big spread leads to a greater **uncertainty**.

The degree of uncertainty is often assessed by working out the average results and stating the range.

Example

In a titration experiment the following repeat measurements of a concentration were taken: $72.0g/dm^3$, $72.4g/dm^3$, $71.9g/dm^3$, $72.1g/dm^3$, $71.8g/dm^3$

Calculate the average result and degree of uncertainty.

$$\text{Average result} = \frac{72.0 + 72.4 + 71.9 + 72.1 + 71.8}{5}$$

$$= \textbf{72.04g/dm}^3$$

The range is from $71.8g/dm^3$ to $72.4g/dm^3$.

This gives an overall uncertainty of $0.6g/dm^3$.

$$\text{Percentage error} = \frac{0.6g/dm^3}{72.04g/dm^3} \times 100$$

$$= 0.83\%$$

Certainty is $100 - 0.83 = 99.17\%$

This result may be quoted as **99.17+/- 0.83% certain**.

Systematic and Random Errors

Two general sources of measured uncertainty are…
- **systematic** errors
- **random** errors.

Systematic errors mean that repeat measurements are consistently **too high or low**. This could result from an incorrectly zeroed balance. For example, the scales opposite show a reading of 0.06 rather than 0.00.

All repeats for the experiment would be incorrect by the same amount.

Random errors…
- mean that repeat measurements give **different values**
- can be introduced when the meniscus isn't on the calibration line
- are one-off errors and wouldn't be the same for all repeats.

Systematic Errors

Random Errors

Meniscus

Calibration line at 25cm³

Quick Test

1. When performing a titration, why is it important to collect more than one result?
2. How do you convert cm³ to dm³?
3. Name two types of error.

C7 Exam Practice Questions

1. Look at the displayed formulae shown below.

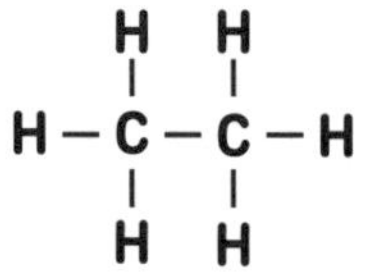

```
    H   H                  H   H              H   H
    |   |                  |   |              |   |
H — C — C — H          C = C          H — C — C — O — H
    |   |                  |   |              |   |
    H   H                  H   H              H   H

   Ethane                Ethene              Ethanol
```

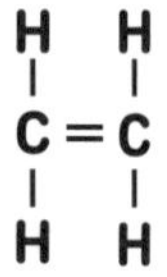

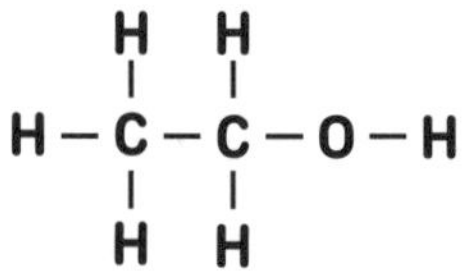

(a) (i) Which of the compounds above is an alcohol? [1]

_____

(ii) Which of the compounds above is unsaturated and would decolourise bromine water? [1]

_____

(iii) Which of the compounds above could be used to make a plastic through the process of polymerisation? [1]

_____

(iv) Which of the compounds above could react with a carboxylic acid to form an ester? [1]

_____

(b) Ethanol can be produced by fermenting grape juice using yeast.

(i) Why isn't it possible to make a concentrated solution of ethanol by fermentation? [1]

_____

(ii) Name the method used to concentrate the alcohol to make spirits like brandy and whisky. [1]

_____

(iii) In addition to fermentation, ethanol can be produced using two other methods. Describe these methods and suggest why some people think that one of them isn't environmentally sustainable. [6]

🖉 _The quality of written communication will be assessed in your answer to this question._

_____

_____

_____

_____

_____

_____

2 Ammonia is a bulk chemical made by the reaction of nitrogen with hydrogen. The reaction is reversible, forming a dynamic equilibrium.

$$N_2 + 3H_2 \rightleftharpoons 2NH_3$$

(a) The graph below shows how the percentage yield of ammonia changes with temperature and pressure.

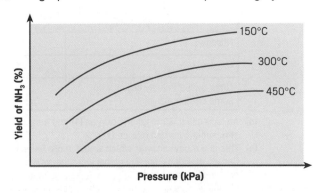

(i) What is the effect of increasing the pressure on the yield of ammonia? **[1]**

_____

(ii) What is the effect of increasing the temperature on the yield of ammonia? **[1]**

_____

(b) Typically, the yield of ammonia in the gas mixture leaving the Haber process reactor is about 20–30%. Eventually all the hydrogen and nitrogen is converted to ammonia. Explain how this is achieved. **[1]**

_____

HT **3** Methane is a fuel that is used in laboratories and in domestic central heating. When it burns in plenty of oxygen, complete combustion occurs, as shown by the following symbol equation:

$$CH_4 + 2O_2 \longrightarrow CO_2 + 2H_2O$$

The table shows the energy required to break each of the bonds involved in the reaction.

Bond	C–H	O=O	C=O	H–O
Energy (kJ/mol)	435	496	805	463

The energy used when the bonds in the reactants are broken can be calculated as follows:

$4 \times$ C–H $= 4 \times 435 = 1740$kJ/mol
$2 \times$ O=O $= 2 \times 496 = 992$kJ/mol
Energy used $= 1740 + 992 = 2732$kJ/mol

(a) Calculate the energy released when the new bonds in the products are made. **[3]**

_____

_____

(b) Calculate the overall energy change for the reaction. **[1]**

_____

Answers

Module C1: Air Quality

Quick Test Answers

Page 5

1. 78% nitrogen, 21% oxygen, 1% other gases (mainly argon with small amounts of other gases including water vapour and carbon dioxide).
2. The early atmosphere of carbon dioxide and water vapour formed from volcanoes. Atmospheric water vapour condensed to form the oceans. Photosynthetic organisms used up carbon dioxide and released oxygen. Carbon dioxide dissolved in the oceans and formed sedimentary rocks and fossil fuels.
3. Photosynthesis and dissolving in the oceans

Page 9

1. Combustion is when a fuel reacts with oxygen (to release energy).
2. A hydrocarbon is a compound made only from carbon and hydrogen.
3. Using less electricity; Removing sulfur from the fuel being used; Removing sulfur dioxide and particulates from the gases released by the power station.
4. **Any four from:** More efficient engines; Low-sulfur fuels; Catalytic converters; Using public transport more; Legal limits for emissions
5. Atmospheric nitrogen is oxidised by atmospheric oxygen at high temperatures to form nitrogen monoxide (NO), which is further oxidised to form nitrogen dioxide (NO_2).

Exam Practice Answers

1. (a) Over time / Between 1990 and 2010 / As the years went on, the concentration of sulfur dioxide [1] decreased [1].
   (b) The introduction of congestion charging in the city centre; More cars were fitted with catalytic converters; **and** Laws were passed to reduce the amount of sulfur in petrol and diesel **should be ticked**.
   (c) Sulfur impurities in fuel [1] react with oxygen [1]. Sulfur dioxide reacts with rainwater [1].

   (d) **Any two from:** High temperature [1] causes atmospheric nitrogen [1] to react with oxygen [1].
2. (a) No actual data was collected at the time / No humans were alive then.
   (b) carbon dioxide **and** water vapour **should be ringed**.
   (c)

Gas	Percentage
Nitrogen	78
Oxygen	21
Other gases (mainly argon, with some carbon dioxide)	1

   (d) An increase in atmospheric oxygen [1] and a decrease in atmospheric carbon dioxide [1].
   (e) **This is a model answer which would score full marks:** Carbon dioxide is causing global warming, which scientists believe will cause flooding of low-lying countries. Sulfur dioxide is causing acid rain, which can damage trees. Nitrogen oxides from car exhausts can cause breathing problems.
   A good answer could also include the following points: Carbon monoxide is a poisonous gas that prevents blood from carrying oxygen; Particulate carbon can cause breathing problems and make buildings dirty.
3. (a) **Any suitable answer that gives the idea of clean emissions, e.g.** It doesn't produce carbon dioxide; It doesn't cause global warming; It produces only water. **Or:** It's renewable.
   (b) **Any two from:** Hydrogen / gas is difficult to store; Hydrogen is difficult to transport; Hydrogen isn't easily available at fuel stations; Hydrogen is flammable or explosive; Hydrogen must be produced from water by electrolysis.

Module C2: Material Choices

Quick Test Answers

Page 14

1. Natural materials: **Any two suitable answers, e.g.** Silk; Wool; Cotton; Paper
   Synthetic materials: **Any two suitable answers, e.g.** Plastics such as poly(ethene); Polyesters; Nylon; PET
2. Fractional distillation
3. The larger the molecule, the stronger the intermolecular forces and the more energy that is needed to overcome the forces, so the higher the boiling point.
4. Fuel for aeroplanes / central heating / camping lanterns.

Page 17

1. Cross-linking makes a plastic stiffer and harder and it increases its melting point.
2. A plasticizer is a small molecule that fits between polymer chains and weakens the intermolecular forces, making the polymer more flexible.
3. Nanotechnology is the study and manipulation of very small particles.
4. In sea spray [**accept 'particulate carbon produced by combustion of fuels'.**]

Exam Practice Answers

1. (a) **Any two from:** Wool; Cotton; Silk; Linen
   (b) PCBD **should be ringed**.

   (c) **This is a model answer which would score full marks:** When working in the rain, a police officer would need a jacket that is waterproof and flexible, but also breathable, so PTFE would be the best choice. When working in a situation in which he or she might be stabbed, the police officer should wear clothing made using PAF because the rigid sheets will protect him or her from being injured.
   (d) **Any suitable answer, e.g.** Silver nanoparticles [1] have been added to fabrics to give them antibacterial properties [1]; Carbon nanotubes [1] have been added to sports equipment to make it stronger / stiffer / lighter [1].
2. (a) Hannah
   (b) **Any suitable answer, e.g.** Naphtha [1] is used as a starting point for chemical reactions / as a feedstock / as a raw material / for chemical synthesis [1]; Bitumen [1] is used as tar for roads / roofing [1].
3. (a) When small molecules / monomers [1] are joined together to make very long molecules [1].
   (b) **Any two correct modifications to polymer and subsequent change to property from:** Increasing chain length [1] increases melting point / rigidity [1]; Cross-linking [1] increases melting point / rigidity / prevents melting / (reference to thermosetting plastic) [1]; Adding a plasticizer [1] increases flexibility [1]; Increasing crystallinity [1] increases melting point / rigidity [1].

Answers

Module C3: Chemicals in Our Lives: Risks and Benefits

Quick Test Answers
Page 21
1. Coal, salt and limestone.
2. **Any three from:** Mountain building; Erosion; Sedimentation; Dissolving; Evaporation
3. **Any two from:** As a flavouring and preservative in food; To treat roads in winter; As a source of chemicals.
4. It can cause high blood pressure.

Page 25
1. Hydrogen, chlorine and sodium hydroxide
2. Splitting up a liquid or dissolved compound using electricity.
3. **Any suitable answer, e.g.** To disinfect water; As a bleach; In the manufacture of plastics.
4. **Any suitable answer, e.g.** Each part of the life cycle (production of materials, manufacture, use and disposal) is assessed for impact on resources, energy requirements, and environmental impact.

Exam Practice Answers
1. (a) **Any one from:** Seawater; Underground salt deposits
   (b) Advantage: **Any one from:** Improve flavour; Act as a preservative.
   Disadvantage: **Any one from:** Cause high blood pressure / hypertension; Cause heart disease / a heart attack.
   (c) Hydrogen – Used in the production of margarines – Flammable

Module C4: Chemical Patterns

Quick Test Answers
Page 30
1. They all have similar physical and chemical properties, and they all have one electron in their outer shell.
2. (a) A mass of 1 and a charge of +1.
   (b) Almost zero mass and a charge of -1.
   (c) A mass of 1 and no charge (it's neutral).

Page 33
1. Melting point decreases and reactivity increases going down the group.
2. They react with water to produce alkaline hydroxide solutions.
3. It floats, fizzes and moves around the surface of the water. Hydrogen and potassium hydroxide are produced. The gas ignites to give a purple flame.
4. Its outer electron is further from the nucleus, so it's held less strongly and lost more easily.

Page 37
1. Lithium is the odd one out because the other elements are halogens.
2. The melting point increases and the reactivity decreases.
3. Potassium bromide and iodine
4. Lithium fluoride

Exam Practice Answers
1. (a)

Particle	Relative Mass	Relative Charge
Proton	1	**+**
Neutron	1	**0 / No charge / Neutral**
Electron	Negligible	**–**

[1 mark for each correct row]
   (b) (i) Nucleus (ii) Electron / Electron shell
   (c) The number of protons in an atom.

Chlorine – Used in bleaches and plastics – Toxic
Sodium hydroxide – Used to make soaps – Corrosive
[2 marks maximum for correct lines joining the left-hand boxes to the middle boxes; 2 marks maximum for correct lines joining the middle boxes to the right-hand boxes.]
2. (a) Making the material **[1]**, manufacturing the product **[1]**, using the product **[1]**, then disposing of the product **[1]**.
   (b) To ensure the results are reliable / consistent.
3. (a) Oxygen can't pass through the film; Transparent; **and** Water can't pass through the film **should be ticked**.
   (b) (i) It could have been toxic / harmful / bad for people.
   (ii) **Any suitable answer, e.g.** Stop using cling film; Only use cling film for foods that don't contain fats or oils.
   (iii) **This is a model answer which would score full marks:** The scientists would find out from a large sample of people how many of them had suffered health problems that might have been caused by plasticizers, and they would find out how often the people had used cling film in recent years. The scientists would carry out an experiment to find out if plasticizers dissolve in oily and fatty foods when they're covered with or wrapped in cling film. They would test plasticizers on animals or human volunteers to find out if they cause health problems.
4. (a) **Accept any value from 12 to 14 inclusive.**
   (b) Lithium carbonate + Hydrochloric acid ⟶ Lithium chloride **[1]** + Carbon dioxide **[1]** + Water **[1]**
   (c) $LiOH + HNO_3 \longrightarrow LiNO_3$ **[1]** $+ H_2O$ **[1]**

(d) (i) Sophie **should be ringed**.
   (ii) Chlorine + Sodium ⟶ Sodium chloride **[1 mark for correct reactants (in either order); 1 mark for correctly named product (not 'NaCl').]**
2. (a) The alkali metals
   (b)

Element	Melting Point (K)	Boiling Point (K)	Formula of Chloride
Lithium	453	**Accept any answer from 1250–1350**	LiCl
Sodium	370	1156	**NaCl**
Potassium	**Accept any answer from 280–350**	1032	KCl

   (c) **Any two from:** It floats; Gas is produced; It moves around on the surface; There is a vigorous reaction.
   Sodium + Water ⟶ Sodium hydroxide + Hydrogen **[1]**
   pH 11/12/13/14 **[1]**
   (d) Flammable **[1]**. Keep away from sources of ignition / heat / fire / Bunsen burner **[1]**.
3. (a) Protons: 9; Electrons: 9; Neutrons: 10
   (b) $F_2(g) + 2Na(s) \longrightarrow 2NaF(s)$
   [1 mark for correct formulae of products and reactants; 1 mark for correct state symbols; 1 mark for a balanced equation.]
   (c) **This is a model answer which would score full marks:** At the start of the experiment, the lamp wouldn't light up because ionic substances don't conduct electricity when solid. This is because the ions are fixed in place. As the solid lead fluoride melts, the ions would become free to move and so the molten lead fluoride would conduct electricity. Therefore the lamp would light up.

Answers

Module C5: Chemicals of the Natural Environment

Quick Test Answers
Page 42
1. The hydrosphere is the term used for the water and dissolved salts on Earth.
2. 21%
3. **Any two from:** It has a high melting point; It's hard; It's insoluble in water.
4. **Any two from:** They have a high melting point; They have a high boiling point; They don't conduct when solid; They conduct when molten or if dissolved.

Page 47
1. Add sodium hydroxide solution and see what colour the precipitate is.
2. Add barium nitrate solution. A white precipitate identifies sulfate ions.
3. The positive ions move towards the negative electrode where they gain electrons. The negative ions move towards the positive electrode where they lose electrons.
4. Positive electrode: oxygen
   Negative electrode: aluminium
5. $Fe^{3+}(aq) + 3OH^-(aq) \longrightarrow Fe(OH)_3(s)$

Exam Practice Answers
1. **(a)** Add sodium hydroxide solution to test for copper ions **[1]** and expect to see a blue precipitate **[1]**. Add silver nitrate solution to test for chloride ions **[1]** and expect to see a white precipitate **[1]**.

(b) Carbonate ion **[1]**. Carbon dioxide **[1]**.
2. **(a)** The ions are able to move apart **[1]** and change to a random arrangement / gain energy / move faster **[1]**.
   (b) oxygen; bottom / cathode; oxygen; top **[2 marks for all four correct; 1 mark for two correct.]**
   (c) **This is a model answer which would score full marks:**
   Aluminium is used for saucepans because it's a good conductor of heat and has a high melting point. Metals have high melting points because of the strong forces of attraction in the lattice structure. Aluminium is used for power lines because it's strong and conducts electricity well. Aluminium is used in aeroplanes because it's strong and lightweight and doesn't corrode. Aluminium is strong because of the tightly packed crystal lattice structure.
   A good answer using higher tier understanding could include the following points: Aluminium is malleable because the rows of ions can slide over each other; Aluminium conducts electricity because the delocalised electrons are free to move in one direction when a voltage is applied.
3. **(a)** $Zn^{2+}(aq) + CO_3^{2-}(aq) \longrightarrow ZnCO_3(s)$
   [1 mark for correct charge on zinc ion; 1 mark for correct formulae and balancing; 1 mark for correct state symbols.]
   (b) $Cu^{2+}(aq) + 2OH^-(aq) \longrightarrow Cu(OH)_2(s)$
   [1 mark for correct formula of $Cu(OH)_2$; 1 mark for correct balancing; 1 mark for correct state symbols.]

Module C6: Chemical Synthesis

Quick Test Answers
Page 53
1. Toxic: skull and crossbones
   Flammable: a flame
2. HCl is hydrochloric acid and H_2SO_4 is sulfuric acid.
3. NaOH
4. $MgO + 2HNO_3 \longrightarrow Mg(NO_3)_2 + H_2O$
Page 57
1. 84
2. 75%
3. **Any three from:** Crystallisation; Filtration; Evaporation; Drying in an oven or dessicator
4. Using a titration
5. 88kg
Page 61
1. The amount of product made per unit time.
2. By weighing the reaction mixture; Measuring the volume of gas produced; Observing the formation of a precipitate.
3. To make the chemical more quickly, so that more profit could be made.
4. The reactant particles are closer together, so the collisions are more frequent.
5. Powders have a larger surface area, so collisions are more frequent.
6. **Any three from:** Catalysts speed up reactions; Catalysts aren't used up or chemically changed; Different reactions need different catalysts; Catalysts lower the activation energy.

Exam Practice Answers
1. **(a)** **Accept any answer between 1 and 6.**
   (b) **Citric acid** + Sodium hydrogencarbonate $\longrightarrow$ Sodium citrate + **Water** + **Carbon dioxide**

(c) (i) Magnesium + Hydrochloric acid $\longrightarrow$ Magnesium chloride **[1]** + Hydrogen **[1]**
   (ii) Hydrogen is flammable **[accept 'magnesium chloride may be harmful'.]**
   (iii) Calcium carbonate + Hydrochloric acid $\longrightarrow$ Calcium chloride + Water + Carbon dioxide **[1]**
   Magnesium carbonate + Hydrochloric acid $\longrightarrow$ Magnesium chloride + Water + Carbon dioxide **[1]**
   The products of these reactions aren't toxic or flammable **[1]**.
   A good answer could also include the following point: Both calcium carbonate and magnesium carbonate are insoluble, so if you take too much antacid it will not make your stomach alkaline.
2. **(a) (i)** Hydrogen / H^+
   (ii) Hydroxide / OH^-
   (iii) $H^+(aq) + OH^-(aq) \longrightarrow H_2O(l)$
   [1 mark for correct reactants and product; 1 mark for correct state symbols.]

   (b)
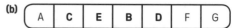

| A | C | E | B | D | F | G |

   [3 marks for all four correct; if incorrect, C before E scores 1 mark, and B before D scores 1 mark.]
3. **(a)** 21–22cm³
   (b) **Any two from:** Increase the concentration of the acid; Increase the surface area of the magnesium carbonate / grind up the magnesium carbonate; Increase the temperature **[accept 'add a catalyst'.]**
   (c) RFM of $MgCO_3$ is 84 **[1]** and RFM of $Mg(NO_3)_2$ is 148 **[1]**. So 8.4g of $MgCO_3$ will make 14.8g of $Mg(NO_3)_2$ **[1]**.

Answers

Quick Test Answers

Page 68
1. Butane
2. —OH
3. Ethanol: solvent or fuel.
   Methanol: chemical feedstock, e.g. in the manufacture of cosmetics.
4. $C_4H_9OH(l) + 6O_2(g) \longrightarrow 5H_2O(g) + 4CO_2(g)$

Page 72
1. Fermentation, synthesis and biotechnology
2. They become denatured and their shape changes permanently, so they no longer work.
3. —COOH
4. An ester

Page 75
1. Endothermic
2. Exothermic
3. Endothermic
4. To remove any unreacted acid.

Page 77
1. Reversible reaction
2. The nitrogen comes from the air. The hydrogen comes from natural gas.
3. To save money and increase the overall yield.

Page 81
1. To ensure that the results are reliable and representative of the substance.
2. Mobile phase is usually water. Stationary phase is paper.
3. R_f value = $\dfrac{\text{Distance travelled by substance}}{\text{Distance travelled by solvent}}$
4. The time taken for a particular substance to pass through the GC column and be detected.

Page 85
1. To ensure that your results are reliable or consistent.
2. Divide by 1000
3. Random error; Systematic error

Exam Practice Answers

1. **(a) (i)** Ethanol
   (ii) Ethene
   (iii) Ethene
   (iv) Ethanol
   (b) (i) The yeast is killed by the alcohol above a certain concentration.
   (ii) Distillation
   (iii) **This is a model answer which would score full marks:**
   In addition to fermentation, ethanol can be produced by synthesis or biotechnology. In synthesis, hydrocarbons from crude oil are cracked to make ethene, which is then reacted with steam under high pressure and temperature in the presence of a catalyst to form ethanol. In biotechnology, *E.coli* are genetically modified by giving them genes that allow them to convert sugars in waste biomass to ethanol. Some people think that synthesis isn't sustainable because it uses products from crude oil, which is a non-renewable resource.

2. **(a) (i)** The yield increases.
   (ii) The yield decreases.
   (b) Unreacted nitrogen and hydrogen are recycled.

3. **(a)** $2 \times C=O = 2 \times 805 = 1610$kJ/mol **[1]**
   $4 \times O\text{-}H = 4 \times 463 = 1852$kJ/mol **[1]**
   Energy released = $1610 + 1852 = 3462$kJ/mol **[1]**
   [A correct answer scores 3 marks.]
   (b) Energy change = Energy used − Energy released
   $= 2732 - 3462$
   $= -730$kJ/mol

Glossary of Key Words

Acid – a compound that has a pH value lower than 7.

Acid rain – rain containing dissolved sulfur dioxide and nitrogen oxides.

Activation energy – the minimum amount of energy required to cause a reaction.

Alkali – a compound that has a pH value higher than 7 and is soluble in water.

Alkali metals – the six metals in Group 1 of the periodic table.

Alkane – a saturated hydrocarbon with the general formula C_nH_{2n+2}

Alkene – an unsaturated hydrocarbon in which there is one or more C=C double bonds.

Atmosphere – the layer of gas surrounding the Earth.

Atom – the smallest chemical particle of an element.

Atom economy – a measure of the amount of reactants in a chemical reaction that end up as useful products; usually expressed as a percentage.

Brine – a solution of sodium chloride in water.

Catalyst – a substance that increases the rate of a chemical reaction without being changed itself.

Catalytic converter – a device fitted to a car exhaust to reduce the emission of air pollutants.

Chemical synthesis – the process by which raw materials are made into useful products.

Chromatography – a technique used to separate different compounds in a mixture according to how well they dissolve in a particular solvent.

Collision theory – a principle that helps to explain rates of reaction. For a reaction to occur, particles must collide with enough energy. Factors that increase the frequency or energy of collisions will speed up a reaction.

Combustion – a chemical reaction that occurs when fuels burn in oxygen, releasing heat.

Compound – a substance consisting of two or more different elements chemically combined.

Covalent bond – a bond between two atoms in which the atoms share one or more pairs of electrons.

Crude oil – a liquid mixture of hydrocarbons found in rocks.

Current – the rate of flow of an electrical charge, measured in amperes (A).

Denatured enzyme – an enzyme that has had its shape destroyed by heat and can no longer catalyse reactions.

Diamond – a form of pure carbon in which each atom is bonded to four other atoms to give a very hard substance.

Diatomic molecule – a molecule that only exists in pairs of atoms.

Displacement – the process that occurs during a chemical reaction when a more reactive element will swap places with a less reactive element within a compound.

Dynamic equilibrium – in a reversible reaction, when the rate of the forwards reaction equals the rate of the reverse reaction.

Electrolysis – the process by which an electric current causes a solution to undergo chemical decomposition.

Electrolyte – the molten or aqueous solution of an ionic compound used in electrolysis.

Electron – a negatively charged particle found orbiting the nucleus of an atom.

Electron configuration – the arrangement of electrons in fixed shells/energy levels around the nucleus of an atom of an element.

Element – a substance that consists of one type of atom.

Endothermic – a chemical reaction that takes in heat from its surroundings so that the products have more energy than the reactants.

Enzyme – a protein that speeds up the rate of a reaction in living organisms (a catalyst in living things).

Erosion – when rocks are broken down by weathering and transported away by water or wind.

Ester – an organic compound that is made by reacting an alcohol and a carboxylic acid.

Evaporation – when a liquid turns into a gas.

Exothermic – a chemical reaction that gives out energy (heat) to its surroundings so that the products have less energy than the reactants.

Fermentation – the process by which yeast converts sugars to alcohol and carbon dioxide through anaerobic respiration.

Fertiliser – a substance added to soil to improve the crop yield.

Fraction – a mixture of hydrocarbons with similar boiling points that is separated from crude oil.

Fractional distillation – the process used to separate the fractions in crude oil using boiling points.

Graphite – a form of pure carbon in which each atom is bonded to three other atoms to create a structure made of sheets that can slide over each other and conduct electricity.

Green chemistry – the production of chemicals based on principles that can lead to a more sustainable process.

Greenhouse gas – gas in the Earth's atmosphere that absorbs radiation and stops it from leaving the Earth's atmosphere.

Group – a vertical column of elements in the periodic table.

Halogen – one of the five non-metals in Group 7 of the periodic table.

Hazard – something that can cause harm. In chemistry, hazards are often chemicals and we use symbols to identify different types of hazard, e.g. flammable, corrosive, etc.

Hydrocarbon – a compound made of carbon and hydrogen atoms only.

Hydrosphere – contains all the water on Earth including rivers, oceans, lakes, etc.

Intermolecular force – the attractive force between two molecules.

Ion – a particle that has a positive or negative electrical charge.

Ionic bond – the process by which two or more atoms lose or gain electrons to become charged ions.

Ionic compound – a compound consisting of charged particles called ions. Ionic compounds are (nearly always) made from a metal and a non-metal.

Life cycle assessment – a multi-step analysis of the environmental impact of an object from manufacture through to disposal.

Lithosphere – the rigid outer layer of the Earth made up of the crust and the part of the mantle just below it.

Mineral – a pure solid element or compound that is found in the Earth's crust.

Monomer – a small hydrocarbon molecule containing a double bond.

Nanometre – a millionth of a millimetre.

Nanoscale – a term used to describe things that happen at a very small scale in which objects are the size of a few atoms.

Nanotechnology – the control and production of materials on a very small scale.

Neutralisation – a reaction between an acid and a base that forms a neutral solution.

Neutron – a particle found in the nucleus of atoms that has no electric charge.

Nucleus – the small central core of an atom, consisting of protons and neutrons.

Ore – a naturally occurring mineral, from which it's economically viable to extract a metal.

Osmosis – the movement of water molecules through a selectively permeable membrane from a dilute solution to a concentrated solution.

Oxidation – the addition of oxygen or the removal of electrons.

Oxidise – to add oxygen to an element or compound, or to remove electrons.

Period – a horizontal row of elements in the periodic table.

Plasticizer – a material added to a plastic to make it more bendy.

Pollutant – a chemical that can harm the environment and health.

Polymer – a giant long-chained hydrocarbon.

Polymerisation – the joining of monomers to make a polymer.

Precipitate – the solid formed in a reaction between two liquids.

Precipitation – a type of reaction in which a solid is made when two liquids are mixed.

Product – the substance made in a chemical reaction.

Property – a descriptive word that can be used when talking about materials and the ways that they behave, e.g. high melting point, good conductor of electricity, etc.

Glossary of Key Words

Proton – a positively charged particle found in the nucleus of atoms.

Qualitative analysis – a form of analysis used to find out whether a substance is present in a sample.

Quantitative analysis – a form of analysis used to find the amount of a substance present in a sample.

Reactant – the substance at the start of a chemical reaction.

Relative atomic mass – the average mass of an atom of an element compared to the twelfth of a carbon atom.

Relative formula mass – the sum of the atomic masses of all atoms in a molecule.

Renewable – a source that will not run out.

Retention time – the time taken for substances to pass through a chromatographic system.

R_f value – a value used in chromatography to identify a substance by comparison with a reference source. It's calculated by dividing the distance travelled by the substance by the distance travelled by the solvent.

Salt – the product of a chemical reaction between a base and an acid.

Saturated (hydrocarbon) – a hydrocarbon molecule with no double bonds.

Sedimentary rock – a type of rock which is made from layers of sediment (mud) that settle out in still water, such as the ocean. Layers build up and are compressed and cemented together.

Sedimentation – when particles of solid that have been carried by a river settle out on the bottom of a river or ocean.

Sodium chloride – also known as 'common salt', this compound is the most abundant compound in seawater and can also be made by reacting sodium with chlorine.

Solvent – a liquid that can dissolve another substance to produce a solution.

Surface area – the area on the outside of a particle that is exposed to another reactant.

Sustainable – capable of being continued with minimal long-term effect on the environment.

Titration – a method used to find the concentration of an acid or alkali.

Unsaturated – a term used to describe alkenes that identifies the presence of a C=C double bond.

Yield – the amount of product obtained from a reaction.

HT **Biofuel** – a fuel that's derived from plant or animal oil rather than from a fossil fuel.

Crystalline – a solid formed by a regular, repeating 3D arrangement of particles.

Distillation – a process used to separate liquids by evaporation followed by condensation to produce a pure liquid.

Reflux – a process of continuous heating without the loss of volatile substances (continuous evaporation and condensation).

Wet scrubbing – when acidic compounds such as sulfur dioxide are removed from power station emission gases by reacting with a solution of an alkali or a mixture of a base and water.

Periodic Table

Key

| relative atomic mass |
| **atomic symbol** |
| name |
| atomic (proton) number |

| 1 | H | hydrogen | 1 |

1	2											3	4	5	6	7	0
																	4 **He** helium 2
7 **Li** lithium 3	9 **Be** beryllium 4											11 **B** boron 5	12 **C** carbon 6	14 **N** nitrogen 7	16 **O** oxygen 8	19 **F** fluorine 9	20 **Ne** neon 10
23 **Na** sodium 11	24 **Mg** magnesium 12											27 **Al** aluminium 13	28 **Si** silicon 14	31 **P** phosphorus 15	32 **S** sulfur 16	35.5 **Cl** chlorine 17	40 **Ar** argon 18
39 **K** potassium 19	40 **Ca** calcium 20	45 **Sc** scandium 21	48 **Ti** titanium 22	51 **V** vanadium 23	52 **Cr** chromium 24	55 **Mn** manganese 25	56 **Fe** iron 26	59 **Co** cobalt 27	59 **Ni** nickel 28	63.5 **Cu** copper 29	65 **Zn** zinc 30	70 **Ga** gallium 31	73 **Ge** germanium 32	75 **As** arsenic 33	79 **Se** selenium 34	80 **Br** bromine 35	84 **Kr** krypton 36
85 **Rb** rubidium 37	88 **Sr** strontium 38	89 **Y** yttrium 39	91 **Zr** zirconium 40	93 **Nb** niobium 41	96 **Mo** molybdenum 42	[98] **Tc** technetium 43	101 **Ru** ruthenium 44	103 **Rh** rhodium 45	106 **Pd** palladium 46	108 **Ag** silver 47	112 **Cd** cadmium 48	115 **In** indium 49	119 **Sn** tin 50	122 **Sb** antimony 51	128 **Te** tellurium 52	127 **I** iodine 53	131 **Xe** xenon 54
133 **Cs** caesium 55	137 **Ba** barium 56	139 **La*** lanthanum 57	178 **Hf** hafnium 72	181 **Ta** tantalum 73	184 **W** tungsten 74	186 **Re** rhenium 75	190 **Os** osmium 76	192 **Ir** iridium 77	195 **Pt** platinum 78	197 **Au** gold 79	201 **Hg** mercury 80	204 **Tl** thallium 81	207 **Pb** lead 82	209 **Bi** bismuth 83	[209] **Po** polonium 84	[210] **At** astatine 85	[222] **Rn** radon 86
[223] **Fr** francium 87	[226] **Ra** radium 88	[227] **Ac*** actinium 89	[261] **Rf** rutherfordium 104	[262] **Db** dubnium 105	[266] **Sg** seaborgium 106	[264] **Bh** bohrium 107	[277] **Hs** hassium 108	[268] **Mt** meitnerium 109	[271] **Ds** darmstadtium 110	[272] **Rg** roentgenium 111							

Elements with atomic numbers 112–116 have been reported but not fully authenticated

*The lanthanoids (atomic numbers 58–71) and the actinoids (atomic numbers 90–103) have been omitted.

The relative atomic masses of copper and chlorine have not been rounded to the nearest whole number.

Data Sheet

Qualitative Analysis

Tests for Positively Charged Ions

Ion	Test	Observation
Calcium Ca^{2+}	Add dilute sodium hydroxide	A white precipitate forms; the precipitate does not dissolve in excess sodium hydroxide
Copper Cu^{2+}	Add dilute sodium hydroxide	A light blue precipitate forms; the precipitate does not dissolve in excess sodium hydroxide
Iron(II) Fe^{2+}	Add dilute sodium hydroxide	A green precipitate forms; the precipitate does not dissolve in excess sodium hydroxide
Iron(III) Fe^{3+}	Add dilute sodium hydroxide	A red-brown precipitate forms; the precipitate does not dissolve in excess sodium hydroxide
Zinc Zn^{2+}	Add dilute sodium hydroxide	A white precipitate forms; the precipitate dissolves in excess sodium hydroxide

Tests for Negatively Charged Ions

Ion	Test	Observation
Carbonate CO_3^{2-}	Add dilute acid	The solution effervesces; carbon dioxide gas is produced (the gas turns limewater from colourless to milky)
Chloride Cl^-	Add dilute nitric acid, then add silver nitrate	A white precipitate forms
Bromide Br^-	Add dilute nitric acid, then add silver nitrate	A cream precipitate forms
Iodide I^-	Add dilute nitric acid, then add silver nitrate	A yellow precipitate forms
Sulfate SO_4^{2-}	Add dilute nitric acid, then add barium chloride or barium nitrate	A white precipitate forms

Index